Praise fo...

REAL SIMPL...

As we paddle furiously to keep our chins from dipping below the water-line of our chaotic lives, we reach for help from those who managed to climb into a lifeboat. Books about simplifying our lives are in no danger of being in short supply. After all, who doesn't want a cleaner closet? But *Real Simplicity* is a different kind of lifeboat. It doesn't try to explain why we are drowning or how we might drown with a little more poise. By helping us reconnect with God's dream that we flourish and not merely survive, this book scoops us up and heads for shore. Thank you, Rozanne and Randy.

NICHOLE NORDEMAN, nine-time
Dove Award-winning contemporary
Christian singer-songwriter

This unique and personal book reveals the secret to a meaningful life in which authentic relationships, family connectedness, and genuine Christianity replace chaotic busyness. *Real Simplicity* moved me from inspiration to transformation.

CAROL KENT, speaker and author
of *Between a Rock and a Grace Place*

For a few years I had the joy of being a neighbor to Rozanne and Randy —with a firsthand experience of their authentic community, including family dinners, neighborhood basketball games, and just hanging out while they grilled on the patio. This book is filled with wisdom and delightful ideas to transform our hectic pace into a life-giving rhythm. And I can't wait to try out Rozanne's recipes!

NANCY BEACH, champion for the arts,
Willow Creek Association,
and television producer,
Front Porch Entertainment

REAL
SIMPLICITY

expanded edition of
~ Making Room for Life ~

ROZANNE & RANDY FRAZEE

ZONDERVAN.com/
AUTHORTRACKER
follow your favorite authors

ZONDERVAN

Real Simplicity
Copyright © 2011 by Rozanne and Randy Frazee

Formerly *Making Room for Life*
Copyright © 2003 by Randy Frazee

This title is also available as a Zondervan ebook.
Visit www.zondervan.com/ebooks.

Requests for information should be addressed to:

Zondervan, *Grand Rapids, Michigan* 49530

This edition: ISBN 978-0-310-33295-4 (softcover)

The Library of Congress has cataloged the original edition as follows:

Frazee, Randy.
    Making room for life: trading chaotic lifestyles for connected relationships /
Randy Frazee. — 1st ed.
        p.   cm.
    Includes bibliographical references.
    ISBN 978-0-310-25016-6 (hardcover)
    1. Christian life. 2. Family — Religious life. I. Title.
BV4526.3F73   2004
    284.4 — dc22   2003017825

Cover design: Michelle Lenger
Cover photography: Veer®
Interior design: Beth Shagene

Printed in the United States of America

11 12 13 14 15 16 /DCI/ 23 22 21 20 19 18 17 16 15 14 13 12 11 10 9 8 7 6 5 4 3 2 1

To Al and Joan Bitonti
(Rozanne's parents).
You taught us and modeled for us that
everything we are and own belongs to God.
Your home and table have always been open to anyone
and filled with food, family, friends, and fun!

Lungo vive il convito!!

Contents

Foreword

Our society is breaking the speed limit. Faster, faster. Tight turns on sharp corners. Accelerator pressed. Tires screaming. White-knuckle grip on the steering wheel.

Is this any way to live? More hours. Extra meetings. Another event. One more trip. Longer commutes. Go! Go! Go!

Whew. Husband and wife fall into bed exhausted and spent, with just enough energy to set the alarm clock so the race can begin again in seven hours.

The human race. I don't know anyone who wins it. But I know a family who pulled out of it. Randy and Rozanne Frazee have learned to slow down. Their lives are not a blur. Their calendars aren't overpacked. Through careful and methodical steps, they have found balance.

And my wife and I are trying to learn from them. We serve together in a large church in one of America's fastest-growing cities. We are tempted to press the gas. But our dear friends Randy and Rozanne are teaching us a much better way. They can teach you as well. Let them. You'll be glad you did.

Max and Denalyn Lucado, San Antonio, Texas

A Word from Randy

In 2003, I wrote a book titled *Making Room for Life*. This book—it was really a journal—was born out of a serious crisis in my life that left me tired, anxious, and depressed. My days were running together; my nights ticked along at a painfully slow pace. I was in a pit and didn't know how to get out.

Francis Bacon wrote, "If you don't apply new remedies, you must expect new evils to emerge." I was staring my new evil in the face with a desperate willingness to apply a new remedy. Radical change was on the offense for a change. In paying attention to the Bible and to my doctor, I discovered a new, yet ancient pathway to a life worth living.

When I shared my story and my new remedy in a Father's Day message at the congregation I served, I discovered I was not alone. There is something in the drinking water of the American lifestyle that, if swallowed, produces amazingly similar symptoms in all of us eventually. This ultimately led to the wonderful opportunity of putting my thoughts in a book.

The road trip of my life has included the most wonderful friend imaginable. Her name is Rozanne. We first started sitting together in church at the age of fifteen. This year we celebrate our thirtieth wedding anniversary. She was there for me during those two difficult years of pain and recovery. She even confessed that, though it was hard to watch me struggle, she somewhat enjoyed a needy and clingy husband for a while. But more than just the difficult years, we have been together for the many great ones. For years now, we have not just been planning to make room for life; we have been soaking it up every single day.

Rozanne has much to say about this topic. I am delighted that the opportunity has come for her voice to enter the conversation, and I am super excited that you are about to take in her pearls of wisdom and nuggets of knowledge as you catch a glimpse of her passion for life.

Our prayer for you is not complicated. It is "real simple." We desire that you won't let another day go by without taking hold of the precious life that God has made available to you. We pray that something we have written in this little book will give you a practical idea, or even the courage to seize the day.

Randy Frazee

A Word from Rozanne

The other day, I woke up with this book in mind and wondered what in the world my friends think a life of real simplicity is. So I promptly logged in to my rarely used Facebook account and changed my status to "Hey friends, tell me what makes (or keeps) your life simple. I would love to hear from you. May you have a wonderfully simple day!" Well, hear back I did. Most of the answers I received were "spending time with my heavenly Father in his Word." "Sabbath." "Dependence on God." Well, what should I have expected? After all, the person asking them was a pastor's wife (one of the many hazards of being friends with a PW). Of course these are the right answers. And really, I do agree with these answers, and I know the friends who gave them practice these habits regularly. And so, even in the midst of feeling guilty for those days when my quiet time is pushed aside for what seems to be more urgent matters, I knew that truthfully their answers are what I want more time for in my life.

However, the one answer that resonated most with me was "good coffee in the morning!" As I read those words posted from my next-door neighbor I felt my muscles begin to relax from my head to my toes. Perhaps I should have phrased the question to require more practical answers. I know what I want in my simple life, but I don't know how to get to it. It's always one chore or errand away, and sometimes I wonder if I will know how to behave when I achieve it.

Why did the coffee answer resonate with me? Well, first of all, my husband, Randy, will tell you we can drive into a town we've never visited before, and I can sniff out the Starbucks. I can even tell you the shopping center it is in before we get close enough to see the signs! Embarrassing, but true. I do love a good cup of coffee. The second reason is that a good cup of coffee is my symbol for taking time to sit and relax—visiting with a friend or perhaps accomplishing a task. Any task instantly becomes more enjoyable and less stressful while I am enjoying that warm cup of java. It offers little breaks in the middle of my work as I pause to take a sip, and sometimes it even causes me to sit down to do a task I might normally accomplish while standing. So what is it for you? What keeps your life simple? If you're scarfing down an espresso because it's faster than downing a whole cup of coffee, then this book is for you!

After seventeen years of living lives of real simplicity, Randy and I still must be intentional about not making decisions that allow us to slip back into the chaos again. Our family, right down to our two-year-old granddaughter, is reaping the benefits of living a deliberately simple life. So grab a cup of coffee (or Diet Coke), sit down with this book, take a deep breath, and let's get started. If you'd like to try a new drink in honor of your quest for a simpler life, use the easy recipe on the next page to create a real treat. I am filled to the brim with enthusiasm for you to experience life as you know it should be—*real simple*.

Rozanne Frazee

Simple Spiced Coffee

5 cups of water *(more if you like weaker coffee)*
½ cup strong ground coffee *(whatever kind you like)*
1 teaspoon ground cinnamon
⅛ teaspoon ground cloves
¼ teaspoon ground nutmeg
¼ cup unpacked brown sugar *(can substitute Splenda brown sugar)*
whipped cream topping *(or regular cream to save calories)*

Mix ground coffee, cinnamon, cloves, nutmeg, and brown sugar together and put in filter basket. Pour water into coffee maker and brew. When coffee is done, pour into cups and top with whipped cream. Relax and enjoy!

Rozanne

PART 1

THE PROBLEM

Squeezing Living Out of Life

Crowded Loneliness
Managing Too Many Worlds

Consider the average day of a typical middle-class family in America. The family rises at 6:00 a.m. Everyone fends for himself or herself for breakfast, while Mom unloads the dishwasher—mostly glasses, since a home-cooked meal hasn't happened for several weeks now. She quickly puts together lunches for the boys and throws the baseball uniforms —washed last night before she went to bed—in the dryer. Dad heads out at 6:45 to beat the 7:00 traffic. His normal commute without excessive traffic is forty-five minutes. Mom and the two children are out the door by 7:15 (usually someone is a little cranky). Mom drops off her elementary-age sons at school by 7:40. Twenty minutes later she arrives at her workplace.

At 3:30 p.m. the children are done with school and enter an after-school program. Mom skips lunch so she can rush out of the office to pick up the kids by 5:00. She runs through the bank teller window and stops at the grocery store on the way home, since before leaving home she had noticed they were running low on milk. She arrives home at 5:45. Fifteen minutes later one son has baseball practice. With barely enough time to get the milk in the fridge, she gets both kids back in the car and rushes to make it to the practice field on time. The other son has a game at 8:00. She calls her husband on the cell phone while taking her son to baseball practice to make sure he can grab the second child at the field and get him to his game by 7:30.

Dad leaves the office at 6:00 p.m., unsuccessful in his efforts to make it through his to-do list. Traffic is now an issue. The forty-five-minute commute stretches into an hour and fifteen minutes. He arrives at the practice field at 7:15 with all the signs of road stress. He kisses his wife, waves to his son in center field, whooshes the second son into the SUV (a mere $700 a month), and heads to the game field about fifteen minutes away. Son #1 finishes practice at 7:30, and he and Mom head for home. On the way they stop at Taco Bell for dinner. They arrive home at 8:00. The boy turns to video games while Mom starts another load of laundry and checks the e-mail.

Meantime, the baseball game gets started late and doesn't end until 9:45 p.m. Dad is still in his business casual clothes, but he does appreciate the forced break to watch his son play ball. On their way home they make a quick stop at the McDonald's drive-through window. They arrive home at 10:30. Once in the house, son #2 reveals that he hasn't finished studying for the math test he's supposed to take tomorrow.

After forty-five minutes of shoving facts into her son's short-term memory while he inhales a McDonald's "Happy" Meal, Mom sends him to bed. It is now 11:15 p.m. Time for bed. Mom and Dad flop into bed, dead tired. They watch a little television; exchange a few words — mostly action items for the next day — and then lights go out. Mom falls asleep as soon as the lights are out. Dad, on the other hand, doesn't. He lies there thinking about all the things that must be done. He knows he needs to sleep, so he gets up and swallows a sleeping pill. It seems to be the only way he can get a good night's sleep lately. It bothers him a little, but he doesn't see any alternative. Tomorrow promises more of the same. Things seem a little harried and out of hand, but the following assumptions keep the family from making any changes:

- Everyone lives this way.

- This is a privileged life that can only be maintained with hard work and discretionary money.

• Things will even out soon. This is just a temporary season of busyness.

Maybe this mirrors your life. The activities may be different, but the movement and noise are the same. The initial thought is that the more financial resources you have, the more likely you are to have a stress-free, relaxing life. In reality, though, studies show that with increased resources comes increased complexity, not simplicity. If they aren't especially careful, the ones who have more actually have more with which to destroy themselves.

Maybe you can relate to the cartoon caption below. Can you think of how many times you've made a resolution to do something about busyness and stress in your life only to find nothing really changing?

"Fred, you must learn to relax."

Noise and movement make up so much of our lives that we don't know how to effectively stop when a little R & R is attempted. There is among Americans a common illness called "leisure sickness."[1] This malady manifests itself in several forms, such as flulike symptoms, headache, sore throat, and muscle aches. Essentially, our bodies and emotions are so stressed out during the week that in the evenings and particularly on the weekends we fall apart. The only prescription for this social fever is a change in lifestyle.

I am a pastor in a large church, a husband, and the father of four children. The opportunities to send myself into the "rubber room" of insanity abound. Preparing sermons, managing staff, meeting parishioners' expectations, tending to constant changes that need to be implemented, spending time with family, paying individual attention to each of my children, having individual time with my wife, exercising, staying in touch with my extended family, helping with science projects, going to children's sports events — the list goes on and on. I don't know how many times people have approached me with the words "I'm concerned about you; you have too much to handle." I think I lived so long under extreme stress that I lost sense of what was happening. It had become routine and normal. This is a scary place to be.

So the impetus for my initial search for connectedness or community was not a need to prepare a sermon or write a book but a need for personal sanity. I knew I couldn't obtain connectedness by increasing my speed or extending my hours of work. King Solomon tried it about three thousand years ago and found out that it doesn't work. I'm nowhere close to being the smartest guy in the world, but I'm smart enough to listen to the world's wisest person.

I needed something fresh, something deeper. I also had a sense of urgency. Several years ago as my daughter approached her sixteenth birthday, I realized I wouldn't have much more time with my children, and I didn't think my health would hold out under the daily pressure I was voluntarily inflicting on it. At the same time I didn't want my life to be meaningless. I didn't want to retire from life and sit in the back-porch rocker watching little birds suck juice out of a jar. I've always lived with a strong sense that God has a calling on my life, that he has something for me to accomplish. But I needed to find some balance and establish some boundaries. Certainly a big part of what God has for my life is what I can *become* as a person in Christ—not just what I *do* for Christ.

The solutions to my dilemma were rooted in God's Word, coupled with the common sense of sages who have gone before us. It has rescued me from a life of running on a hamster's wheel, a life of motion without meaning.

Managing Your Relationships

Let's begin our journey together with some self-discovery. Grab a pen or pencil and a piece of paper. Now look at the following illustration.

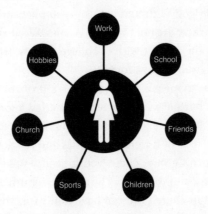

The individual in the center represents a person who is trying to make more room for life. Each of the smaller circles represents a relationship that they manage. They may invest time daily in a particular relationship, or only a few times a year. Think about your life and the various relationships you manage, and draw a circle for each.

When you've completed this, go back to each circle you have drawn and ask yourself the question, "Is that really one relationship group, or are there more worlds within each circle that are managed separately?" For example, if you have more than one child, do they go to the same school? If not, then you need to draw a separate circle for each school. If you are married, does your spouse work? If you don't both work at the same place, then you need to draw an additional circle representing this separate relationship. If you have children, are they involved in sports? If so, are they involved in multiple sports like soccer, baseball, and volleyball? What about music lessons? How about extended family? You should already have a circle representing your family and another circle representing your spouse's family. Do they all live in the same town, or are they spread throughout different states? If they are in different cities or states, then you need to draw a circle for each one. Are you in a blended family situation? If there is joint custody, then you need to draw a circle for each relationship. How about your hobbies? Maybe you have a group you golf with and a group you play cards with. Draw a different circle if these are not the same people. What about past friends you try to maintain contact with — college friends, friends you had in other places you lived, and so forth?

If you live in suburban America, you're probably getting a little stressed by now, but please continue on for a few more minutes. Now consider church. If you are involved in a church, is it really one circle, or are there many circles of different activities and relationships (missions committee, women's group, choir, youth group, small group, support group, elder board, and the like)? The average suburban American who is really involved in church life can have four to six different circles. If an entire family is fully involved, there can be as many as fifteen different circles. Draw a circle for each activity or ministry you are involved with. Before you've finished drawing your circles, get some feedback from others about ones you may have overlooked. Be sure to have a circle representing the persons you will ask before you seek their counsel.

Next, you need to consider the line drawn to each circle. These lines represent your commute to these relationships. You may consider drawing an object next to each line that represents the means by which you engage in this relationship. These may be automobiles, airplanes, letters, e-mail, telephones, and so forth. Place a time value on each line representing a round-trip commute to and from that circle. For example, if it takes you an average of forty-five minutes to get to work, write down ninety minutes. I'd invite you to multiply this for the entire month, but it just might put you over the edge.

Now let's consider the issue of commuting in an automobile. Harvard University's Robert Putnam, in his bestselling book *Bowling Alone,* gives some startling statistics on American commuting.[2] His studies show that the average American family engages in thirteen automobile commutes a day! When I first heard this statistic, I immediately dismissed it as not a reality for my family. However, after taking a moment to calculate the average business and school day, I found myself easily within these parameters. To add to the misery, recent studies suggest that 80 percent of cars on the road systems in cities and suburbs in America only have one person in them — the driver.[3] The only source for two-way interaction is either the unwholesome hand gestures exchanged when one is cut off or the cell phone.

Robert Putnam suggests this formula: For every ten minutes you spend in an automobile, you reduce your available social capital (time for relationships) by 10 percent.[4] If his calculations are accurate, as you look at the drawing of your social world you may conclude that not only do you not have any social capital available at the end of the day; you are going into social debt. If you believe we are created as social beings who require a quantity (and a quality) of people interaction each day to survive, then this means we are dying — not from physical illnesses only but from social illness as well. I'm quite confident, as historians look back on this era, one of the marks we will bear is *the death of community and perhaps even of the family*.

Many people turn to the church to solve their problem of loneliness and disconnectedness. Because the church has been commissioned by

Christ to reach out and to develop a functioning community, it is an appropriate place to turn. The church's principal solution for community over the last thirty to forty years has been the small group. Without question, the small group movement has made its mark on society. Studies show that 40 percent of Americans are involved in some kind of small group.[5] Many people get involved in such a group to find a point of connection and a greater sense of intimacy and belonging, to have a place where they can share fears and dreams. Testimony reveals that small groups are good and helpful. But studies also show that they often don't work.[6]

Thinking of the old Chinese proverb that states "the beginning of wisdom is to call something by its right name," go back to your personal galaxy and add a circle for your small group (if you haven't already).

I love to cook, and over the years, I have established a favorite ingredient. The lemon. Fresh lemon juice is used in almost every meal I make, whether I splash it on chicken, fish, vegetables, potatoes, sauces, salads, or desserts. The juice of a lemon can wake up and brighten the flavors of almost any food. However, my favorite thing to do is to simply squeeze and then drop a wedge into my water. Mmmm! So much more refreshing than plain water, and I drink more of it.

One evening, I saw a lemon lying on the counter that I had used to flavor my broccoli. As I picked it up and examined it, I realized I had squeezed the life out of that lemon. The pulp was smashed to the sides, the fresh juice gone, and the only thing left was the bitter rind. Suddenly it dawned on me. I felt like that lemon! The busyness and craziness of managing my worlds and those of each of our four children, being involved in our church life and our interest groups, experiencing life with our extended family and our friends, had squeezed the life right out of me. I was nothing more than a shell of a lemon — insides smashed,

---

Now rename the small group according to what you see and feel. How about "Another World to Manage"? The fault does not lie with the concept of smallness or with the people. The problem lies with *orbit management*. Most people confess to rushing from one world to a totally separate world of small group. In other words, the people in their small groups are not involved in any other group they manage. Very few small group members get together outside of the formal meeting date, not because there isn't a desire, but because there just isn't any time. While attempts are made, there is little chance the members of the small group can get their arms around your world or your arms around theirs. Their lives simply do not intersect anywhere except the small group meeting — and perhaps a quick hello at church on Sunday morning. We are simply not principal characters in each other's worlds.

left with bitterness created by our chosen lifestyle. I was accomplishing everything, yet yelling constantly at our kids to hurry up. I was angry at my husband frequently and didn't even really know why. But I didn't think I could stop this craziness we called our life.

Getting pushed aside were exercise, hobbies, and reading (especially my quiet times) — the things that replenished me. If I did stop all the rushing, it meant I'd be letting someone down. Who would it be? My husband? Which of our four children? Besides, I was thinking that my "Mother of the Year" award was just around the corner, if only I could keep it up for a little while longer. (Yes, at times it was all about me.) So I sustained and perpetuated our insane rat race, all the while becoming an angry and bitter shell of a person, just like my squished lemon sitting on the counter. Are you feeling a little like a squeezed lemon, insides squished and dry, with nothing left but the bitter rind? If you do, keep reading, because there is an alternative.

Rozanne

If you haven't done so already, finish drawing your worlds, or add new ones that came to mind as you read. What are your thoughts about what you have drawn? If you're the average person, you'll be seeing a picture of stress. Take some time to give the right name to your life. How about "Lost in Space" or "Everybody Knows My Name, but Nobody Knows Me" or "Planet Hopper" or "Space Shuttle Dweller"? How about a new name for your car such as "Cocoon on Wheels" or "Mobile Penitentiary Cell"? If we are going to experience real simplicity, if we are going to make room for life, these are the kinds of honest confrontations with our existing lifestyles that we must have.

As you read the following pages and think through the implications for your life, be sure to formulate a list of action steps that will move you further from *mere existence* and closer to *authentic living*. My goal and passion are not just to see you exist in a life of crowded loneliness but to give you a vision for a new way of life — along with practical steps to get there. The ideas will be, I hope, easy to understand, but the implementation will take courage. But if you're like me and so many others I know, you are ready for a change.

|||||||||||||| DISCUSSION AND REFLECTION ||||||||||||||||

1. What does a life of real simplicity mean to you? If you were to become successful at simplifying your life, what would you be doing—and maybe more importantly, what wouldn't you be doing?

2. Discuss the difference between "loneliness" and "crowded loneliness." Which of these do you have a tendency to struggle with more?

3. Look at the drawing you made of all your relational worlds. Are your separate relational worlds keeping you from deeper, more satisfying relationships? What steps can you take to address this?

4. Identify one personal action step you can take toward adopting a life of real simplicity.

The Connection Requirement
Created for Community

If we hope to be successful in truly experiencing real simplicity and making room for life, we're going to have to rebuild our current lifestyles on a new foundation. We cannot simply pour more money and energy into the paradigm of crowded loneliness. Managing an endless number of disconnected linear relationships is exhausting. But more than just making us tired, this way of life is toxic.

Those of us who are single or who are married with no children may have an easier time keeping up with relational worlds than those of us who are married with children, especially small children. Through the years, however, we have seen even those who have more freedom get tired of running between relationships. Although they don't understand exactly why, they have not found these disconnected relationships to be as satisfying as they should be. Over time, they have discovered they are looking for something deeper as well.

We were created with a connection requirement, and if this requirement is not satisfied, we will eventually die. If we ever became convinced of this, it would make our pursuit of a simpler relational life a higher priority. This, then, is the goal of this chapter.

"We" versus "Me"

North Americans have a reverence for individuality and consumerism. It flows from the teaching of men like René Descartes, who popularized the phrase "I think, therefore I am." At first this seems like a rather benign and esoteric philosophic phrase. Its most basic meaning suggests that one's identity flows from oneself. After all, Whitney Houston sang that to love oneself was "the greatest love of all." Without boundaries, Americans have taken the concept of self-identity to a new level afforded them by wealth. In America, success is defined by the next purchase. In many places around the world, success is defined by a simple meal and conversation with family and friends. The accumulation of stuff is added to our "net worth" statement that deems us "worthy" in relationship to others who have less.

We passionately pursue the next purchase in an attempt to raise our perceived value. These are two very different foundations to build a life on with two very different results. We now live by the phrase "I purchase/accumulate, therefore I am."

In one of their "Strange but True" columns titled "Selling the 'me' versus 'we,'" brothers Rich and Bill Sones answered this question: "How are ads that target consumers in individualistic societies such as the United States and Canada different from ads in communal societies such as Korea?"

> The former try to sell EGO and what the product can do for you; the latter sell SOCIAL CONNECTEDNESS and how the product can foster feelings of belonging and harmony ...
>
> "Be all that you can be. Join the Army," is a classic U.S. pitch at individualistic ego-enhancement. Toyota's "I love what it does for me. From any angle" (the car pictured front and sideways) succeeds in the U.S., but "The best relationships are lasting ones ... Toyota Quality" works better in communal Korea. When researchers Sang-Pil Han and Sharon Shavitt tested chewing gum ads in both cultures, they found "Treat yourself to a breath-freshening

At the top of the list for most parents is the desire to provide a good house in a good neighborhood. Both parents have entered the workforce to give their children two main things — safety and education. Let me explain. First and foremost most parents want to see their children attend the right school, so they mortgage both their incomes to buy a house that is located in a safe neighborhood with desirable schools, or so they can afford private school tuition.

In The Two-Income Trap, *mother and daughter authors Elizabeth Warren and Amelia Warren Tyagi state, "The Two-Income Trap is thick with irony. Middle-class mothers went into the workforce in a calculated effort to give their families an economic edge. Instead, millions of them are now in the workplace just so their families can break even."[1] We will do anything for our kids, and this is a worthy pursuit — as long as what we are pursuing is truly the most important things that our children need.*

While I have nothing against mothers working, my concern comes because of the added stress it places on the family with regard to time and finances. The "trap" comes when a tragedy hits the family — an unexpected expense, job loss (layoff or firing), or major health crisis. The family has played all its cards and has no fallback plan. Approximately one in seven families with children has declared bankruptcy over the last decade.[2] Given our present economy, this number may well rise over the next several years.

Rozanne

experience" worked in one but not the other; the same for "Share a breath-freshening experience." Can you guess which was which?[3]

If you, like most people I know, are worn out from a lifestyle of accumulation, then an invitation to a lifestyle of conversation and community is welcome. Our universal longing for community is a validation in and of itself of the connection requirement. It should make us want to run to this new place.

South African Anglican minister Desmond Tutu has coined a term that exposes a richer foundation for living—one built on community and conversation in contrast to individualism and accumulation. The term is *ubuntu*—African for "people"—and it has come to represent a community theology expressed in the phrase "we are, therefore I am." This powerful phrase suggests that one's identity is formed by community.[4] One of the fundamental beliefs of *ubuntu* can be expressed in the African saying, *motho ke motho ba batho ba bangwe/umuntu ngumuntu ngabant,* which means, "A person can only be a person through others."[5] In other words, our perceived value goes up in proportion to our investment in community. This teaching implies that we were designed with a connection requirement. I further suggest that this belief structure is more in keeping with what God had in mind when he created us.

Created for Connection

How were we made? What are the requirements for living healthy and fruitful lives? Let's draw our attention to the original design of human life in Genesis 1–2 to find the answers. In the six-day description of the creation of the heavens and the earth and all living things within it, God makes a journal entry into his construction log: "It is good." This should not surprise us given the scope and depth of God's capacity. On the sixth day, God unveils his supreme creation—us! With the inclusion of the human being into the equation God makes this final comment in chapter 1: "God saw all that he had made, and it was very good." Trinity Construction engaged in history's ultimate design-build project. I'd love to see the drawings on how one goes about setting the sun, moon, and stars in their proper places.

When we get to chapter 2 of Genesis, the author goes into greater detail on God's design and purpose for man. We are told that God took dust from the ground and formed it into the human shape. Then, he breathed into Adam's lifeless nostrils the "breath of life," and Adam became a living being (verse 7). We are told that God provided a dwelling place for Adam called the garden of Eden (verses 8 – 14). As you read the description of this place, you get the idea that Adam had a home that makes Bill Gates's estate look like a tool shed. We are told that Adam was given the job of caring for the garden — which couldn't have been too hard since weeds hadn't yet been created (3:18). We're also told that Adam was to eat to his heart's content from any of the trees except one — the tree of the knowledge of good and evil (2:16 – 17). What a deal to have only one law to obey. It would never be this simple again.

Then in Genesis 2:18 the unexpected happens. After six consecutive entries of how good things were — the last entry even suggesting that the whole project was very good — we are not expecting God to say that something is not good, but he does. "The LORD God said, 'It is *not good* for the man to be alone' " (verse 18, emphasis added). What does this mean?

If God knew that man could not handle human isolation, why did he not deal with this up front on day six? I believe this is God's way of highlighting for us man's need for community. If God had created Eve on the sixth day, along with Adam, we might have taken for granted the absolute importance of companionship and conversation. I think God delayed the creation of Eve to drive the point home that humans have not been created to be alone. In other words, *community is the only change order in creation.* God is saying that he designed humans to require oxygen to live. By the same token, he is also saying that we must have community to live. We are built with a connection requirement.

"We Theology"

For most of my Christian life, I've read the New Testament letters as though the authors were writing to individuals about growing as individuals in Christ. I took the perspective of American individualism and consumerism and read it into Scripture: "Everything is all about me." After gaining an understanding that the mission of the church is to build up and bring to maturity the body of Christ, which is made up of *all of us*, not just me, I now see that I had been missing the communal purpose of life.

I have a call as an individual to become like Christ in the way I live. This call is empowered by the Spirit of God within me as I yield my life in obedience to God's Word. However, this call must not be seen in isolation, apart from my interaction with other believers. To do so would be like exercising your right arm when you lifted weights but not your left. If you did this over time, your body would begin to look rather lopsided and strange. Together we are to give ourselves to loving God and loving each other. As a unified body, with Christ as the

If you still harbor any doubt that we humans were created with a connection requirement, I suggest you check your cell phone, e-mail, Facebook, My Space, and Twitter accounts before you agree to disagree. (If you don't have all of these accounts, check your kids' accounts; I'm sure they have them.) The Facebook craze started in 2004 when Mark Zuckerberg, a Harvard student, wanted to create a social network of Harvard students. "Although Zuckerberg's intent was networking, it has taken off and become an Internet community," observes John Norvell, a visiting lecturer on cultural anthropology at Scripps College.[6]

I established a Facebook account because I wanted to understand what my children were experiencing and why it was so compelling. Not sure how to do it, I solicited their help. After a couple of hours of trying to create my profile, I hit the friend request button and invited my kids to be my Facebook buddies. To my extreme pleasure (and relief) they all confirmed my request. After spending a couple of hours exploring their profiles, I went to bed as a happy mom. I saw pictures of all their friends and observed their conversations — and all were wholesome. Whew! Until the next morning!

Head, we are to love others outside this community of faith in the hope that they will experience the love of Christ through us and even join us — because Christ's offer is for everyone (Ephesians 4:14 – 16). The Protestantism that drives American Christianity has a streak of "protesting" things like community. Our attitude is often one that promotes rugged individualism over community. When we open the New Testament, we often read it in light of our individualism, reading a "me theology" into what is written. We would do well to learn from our Catholic brothers and sisters who have historically read the Bible from a community perspective, often called a "we theology." We are, after all, created with *a connection requirement.*

After I woke up, I checked my e-mail, and I had 120 Facebook friend requests in my inbox. Of course, I accepted all of them. I didn't want to hurt anyone's feelings by turning them down. I smiled as I added my son's girlfriend, then a boy who lived down the street from us who hung out with my other son. Some of them were my own friends. I didn't even know they were on Facebook! There were many people, however, that I didn't know. They were friends of friends of friends.

With the technology craze, I dare say we are trying to stay connected more than we ever did in past generations. Our cell phones give us the ability to be available 24/7. Facebook and MySpace help us know what's going on in our relationships without even having to converse with people. Then there is Twitter, which allows you to know your friends' every thought — or at least as often as they choose to update their account.

Can you imagine keeping up with all those relationships in person? Our technology has brought us to a new level of crowded loneliness — people all around, including those who pop up to greet us in our inbox, but not an actual face in sight.

Rozanne

Evidence of the Connection Requirement

If it is true that God designed us with a connection requirement, then it would stand to reason that if someone were isolated from connection, it would have serious negative effects on his or her life. The American Institute of Stress has conducted extensive research on the role of social support in health. The findings are conclusive, incessant, and staggering. Directly off the pages of their research reports are these words: "The wisdom of the ages, anecdotal observations, careful clinical case studies and trials, epidemiological data on marriage, divorce and death, as well as sophisticated psychophysiological and laboratory testing—all confirm that strong social support is a powerful stress buster."[7] This summary statement basically says that it doesn't take a medical doctor to conclude that community is essential to life, but if you need this kind of evidence, they'll provide it in spades.

For example, careful research was conducted on 232 patients who had undergone cardiac surgery. Of these patients, twenty-one died within six months. Two statistically significant mortality predictors that emerged from these twenty-one cases were a "lack of participation in social or community groups, and the absence of strength and comfort from religion."[8] The medical community has pondered the strong connection between community and cardiovascular disease and concluded that wholesome community reduces hyperactive cardiovascular reactivity to stress.[9] When this community is spiritually based, health rises even further. Here is a scientific verification that God created us with a connection requirement.

Another example comes from a Swedish report that demonstrates that middle-aged men who had recently endured high levels of emotional stress but had little emotional support were three times as likely to die over the next seven years as those with close personal ties.[10] A California study involving seven thousand men and women found that after nine years those with the fewest social ties were twice as likely to die as those with the strongest ones.[11] The American Institute of Stress also cites a report indicating that social activity can predict cardiac mortality as strongly as elevated cholesterol and serum lipid patterns.[12] Research shows that lack of social support is linked with higher mortality rates for heart attacks, diabetes, rheumatoid arthritis, and other autoimmune disorders.[13] Finally, another well-documented study shows that social isolation contributes to illness and death as much as smoking.[14] So if you feel you must smoke, for goodness' sake, *don't do it alone!*

In this chapter we've learned that we are created with a connection requirement. After reading these first two chapters, many people will nod their heads in agreement, concluding that they possess the social support necessary to satisfy the divine requirement. Most people, as a matter of fact, might even conclude that companionship isn't their particular problem. We have people all around us.

In reality, though, it's possible to be in the company of others and still feel isolated. Community specialists call this brand of isolation experienced by the majority of Americans "crowded loneliness." It is the most dangerous loneliness of all because it emits a false air of community that prevents us from diagnosing our dilemma correctly. We have exposure to people but not a deep connection to people. The truth is that there is a huge gap between God's original design for connection and the way most of us live our lives. Over the last fifty to seventy-five years, Americans and people from other advanced industrialized places either have never understood this design requirement or have downgraded it to an optional amenity. We must dissolve that gap and close it, or we will continue to struggle, suffer, and—I would even dare to suggest—die before our time.

IIIIIIIIIIIIIII DISCUSSION AND REFLECTION IIIIIIIIIIIIIIIIII

1. This chapter suggests we need to make a shift from a lifestyle of accumulation to a lifestyle of conversation. What would this change look like in your life?

2. How do you feel about the evidence that the condition of a person's physical health is connected to their level of relational connectivity? Do you believe that you or those in your network of relationships have physical problems because of a lack of significant community? Identify one step you can take this week to address this issue.

3. Someone has wisely observed, "We don't work to provide for our needs; we work to fund our chosen lifestyle." Be completely honest as you answer these questions: What is the purpose of my work? What am I trying to achieve through my work?

4. Identify one personal action step you can take toward adopting a life of real simplicity.

PART 2

THE SOLUTION

*Restructuring Our Relationships
and Time*

The Secret
of the Bedouin Shepherd

The Solution Is Not
More of the Same

Several years ago, I took my first trip to Israel. Our group traveled on a luxurious tour bus from one ancient city to the next, taking in the wonderful religious and spiritual sites of the Holy Land. In between the cities we would pass by hot, dry desert hills on the left and right. It appears to be the part of the Holy Land that the milk and honey never reached. Even though I was encased in an air-conditioned vehicle, my impulse was to reach for my bottled water and my fifty-block sunscreen.

Intermittently on these various hillsides were the shabby box tents of the Bedouin shepherds. I remember shaking my head and pondering how difficult life must be for them. Each of my four children has their own room equipped with gadgets too embarrassing to speak of here. As I gazed at the tents, they did not appear to have a 4/3/3 configuration (four bedrooms, three baths, three-car garage). I remember studying in seminary about the Bedouin, in connection with the little shepherd boy who found some of the Dead Sea Scrolls in a cave in the ancient Qumran community in 1947. The photographed faces of the men and women in the texts I studied contained deep wrinkles parched by excessive exposure to the sun. The gap in the way of life between those of us on the tour bus and the Bedouin shepherds was enormous. I definitely felt I was the privileged one.

Then our Arab-Christian tour guide grabbed the microphone at the front of the bus and turned my world upside down. He said, "Off to your right you will see the mobile residence of the Bedouin shepherd and his family. Once their livestock has grazed the available vegetation, the family will pick up their humble homes and move to a new place to repeat the cycle." He went on to say that *the average Bedouin lives*

The Bedouin are known for their hospitality. Foundational to their tribal creed is the practice that no traveler is turned away.[1] Their major priorities center around relationships and social life. Hospitality seems to have become a lost art in the pursuit of our American Dream. We can't seem to fit it in amid all our modern conveniences and time-saving devices. But for the Bedouin, it is a mainstay.

We've learned from the Bedouin to share our day around the dinner table. After each person shares how their day has gone from the time they woke up (if you don't say you woke up, then we assume it is all a dream), they are given an opportunity to rate their day on a scale of 1 to 10. (More about this in a later chapter.) Of course there is no right or wrong answer. During this time of sharing, we have an opportunity to ask questions about each person's day so we can gain insight and give encouragement.

We also love to share stories about when our children were little or when my husband and I were young. We have some very special foods that come from our different cultural backgrounds. One is spaghetti, since my family is Italian (my dad and mom were the first generation in the family to have been born in America). Growing up, we had pasta to be over one hundred years old! Without even meaning to, I blurted out, "How can this be?" Abed, the guide, told of a study recently completed by the government of Israel. They were just as curious about the Bedouin's longevity as I was and wanted to get to the bottom of their secret, bottle it, and sell it alongside the mineral-rich mud of the Dead Sea that promises to create youthful skin. It was obvious by looking at them that the Bedouin did not apply the mudpacks to their faces, but they did something far better.

The first hunch was to study the diet of the Bedouin. While it is true that their meals include whole foods, no preservatives, no candy,

---

several times a week. On Thanksgiving, we had turkey and pasta. For Christmas, we had ham and pasta. In the summer time, we had family get-togethers with hamburgers and — you guessed it — pasta!

My husband's family has a simple meal called "Polish Boys." Our kids will ask for this quite often, especially if they are bringing friends home for dinner. They request Polish Boys mostly because, while it is a tasty and unusual meal that Randy's mom adapted from a restaurant entrée recipe, it comes with a story — a story that is as much a part of the experience as the meal itself. My children know that when we have Polish Boys, Dad always tells the story, which intersects his childhood and mine.

Close your eyes and think of a meal that has a special memory for you. Is it from your childhood? Or from more recent times? Recently a blogger named Scott Hutchinson caught my attention as he was interviewed on the radio. One of the things he said went something like this: "I've never heard or read a food memory anyone shared about standing at a tall table in a fast-food restaurant eating a deli sandwich. Almost all of them are about meals that are prepared and shared with family and friends." How about your food memories?

Rozanne

and a moderate intake of meat, this was not the number one cause of the Bedouin's longevity. Abed revealed the secret: *no stress.*

This makes complete sense! Stress makes us sick, drives us crazy, and can kill us some thirty years before a poor shepherd dies at the age of a hundred. Most Bedouin would not change places with us, even if given the opportunity. And why would they? So they can be stressed-out as they run hard to nowhere?

What does the average day in the life of the Bedouin family look like? The family rises from their tents slightly before sunrise so they are ready to capture the precious hours of sunlight. There is just enough sun peering over the horizon to see the objects in front of them. As the

Interestingly enough, in the 1960s, after Israel became established as a state, the mobility of the Bedouin was severely threatened by the growth of cities. In an effort to assist, the Israeli government established planned towns and encouraged the Bedouin families to move into urban settings. The government touted these towns as promoting the overall well-being of families, offering health clinics, schools, and access to running water, electricity, and telephone service. This was an all-out effort to bring the ancient Bedouin culture up-to-date with the twenty-first century. On the surface it seemed benevolent; however, it introduced a host of rapid changes to the ancient practices of our nomadic friends that have proven less than optimal.[2]

Two key changes were related to diet and physical activity. The result of this urbanizing? A major increase in obesity, diabetes, and cardiovascular disease over the 44 percent who retained their traditional lifestyle.[3] *Why? As these former nomads began to assimilate into city life, they had access to modes of transportation previously unavailable to and unnecessary for them. Thus, the Bedouin were welcomed into the ranks of the more hurried lifestyles of their contemporaries. They were no longer* sun comes up, each member of the family has a job to do. Some tend the sheep—the core business of the Bedouin. Some make clothes or prepare for the upcoming meals. Some mend with needle and thread the tears in the tents. At various intervals, the Bedouin make their way to town to barter the wool of their sheep for other staple items such as food and materials.

Whatever work to be accomplished is done during the day before the sun sets. There is no artificial light to expand the workday. Everyone gathers back to the cluster of tents—mother, father, children, grandparents, aunts, uncles. There are no television sets, no phone calls, no e-mails. Each night the family gathers for dinner. They are in no

walking, nor did they have the physical jobs that required the whole family's participation. What's more, their stomachs became filled with store-bought processed foods instead of homegrown fruits and vegetables.

Another factor was that the men were entering the workforce outside their immediate area because jobs were few in those residential towns the government had created, and children began attending schools in neighboring towns as well. Now because family members were away from home for much of the day, the wife and mother, who by tradition was responsible for what her family ate, was no longer in control of what her family consumed, thus allowing introduction of foods high in sugar and fat.

Urban life brought to the Bedouin families all the other stresses experienced in Western civilization. While they quickly joined our ranks of commuting, eating unhealthily, and experiencing the stress-filled life of modernization, one thing remains the same for the Bedouin: They have maintained their priority of hospitality. *I'm afraid the contemporary Western lifestyle of suburbia has been tested once again and found wanting.*

Rozanne

particular hurry. Each evening can involve three to four hours of simply being together. Often a fire is built, and the Bedouin, young and old, gather around it. There may be music and singing and the telling of stories from the past and from the day.

Because so much of the work of the Bedouin is physical, there is no need to squeeze in a trip to the gym across town or an appointment with a personal trainer. They are tired at the end of the day and routinely go to bed at the same time each night. As the young Bedouin shepherd boy lies down, all is quiet and peaceful; there is no incessant noise of city life to contend with. He peers up into the sky filled with constellations. Thoughts of a mighty God swim in his head. These will be his last thoughts as he falls asleep. Some say the slumber of the Bedouin is a deep, replenishing sleep that eludes most privileged suburbanites.

Even now, as I write this chapter it is Christmas Day, and I'm stuck in an airport in Charlotte, North Carolina, trying to get my family across the country from Texas to Ohio to be with our extended families for the holidays. We just received news that our flight has been canceled — our second flight canceled today. It's highly probable we'll spend the remainder of this special day in the airport.

I walked into a little bar and grill in the airport called Cheers. Everything looks like it came right out of the set of the famous Boston sitcom. Only one problem: *nobody knew my name.* We were in a strange place; we had a fast-food dinner; and we didn't have a single family member in the entire state of North Carolina with whom to share Christmas. All this for a mere $1,800 in airfare. You really have to have a little discretionary money or air miles to ruin a great holiday. For some reason, I think the Bedouin shepherd would get a bigger laugh about my Christmas experience than anything Shelley Long ever said to Ted Danson!

The Bedouin do not live the hectic life of managing disconnected worlds of shallow linear relationships. A beautiful simplicity and a unity and rhythm with creation extend their lives some thirty years beyond ours. They do not have access to our money or our medications. They have no need for them. The Bedouin are not the only people group that has discovered this kind of life—but it is a life that eludes the American suburbanite, almost as though we weren't invited to the meeting or didn't get the memo. Or could it be that we ignored it?

What is the secret of the Bedouin? They approach *relationships* and *time* in a manner completely different from the way we do. This is their secret. It is a way of life that dances with the rhythm of creation. It is a way of life that is filled with a certain brand of community. It is a way of life that is free from the kind of stress we inflict on our lives and that creates all kinds of emotional and physical health problems that can take us out earlier than the master plan demands.

The way of life I speak of is as old as life itself. It sits plainly on the pages of the first two chapters of the Holy Bible. It is reinforced throughout the remainder of the Scriptures. Very seldom is it overtly discussed, because it was the way life was established. People were born into it and didn't know to call it to our attention. They didn't "know that they knew." We, on the other hand, have lived most of our lives "not knowing that we did not know."

My goal is twofold: to get us to "know that we do not know" and then to move us to the point that we "know that we know." It is probably too optimistic to think that our generation can ever get to the stage of the people of the Bible or the Bedouin shepherd, where we "don't know that we know." But this way of life can be realized by us and by the people around us if we have the vision and the courage.

Make a special note of this: *A lifestyle of real simplicity can't be bought with money.* As a matter of fact, the excessive money of many Americans may be the single greatest obstacle to attaining a stress-free lifestyle. We can have the money to purchase the nicest and most exotic hammock ever made, but it doesn't mean we'll find much rest in it. If we point the next generation to the right path and attempt to actually live in community and reject crowded loneliness, perhaps their children will be rightfully called "the New Bedouin."

In honor of a simple way of life, pick an evening this week to have a sit-down dinner with your family and perhaps invite another family over (or someone in your extended family) and serve this simple meal.

Curried Lamb and Lentil Stew

1½ pounds of lean boned leg of lamb cut into pieces
      (you can substitute lean beef stew meat)

1 tablespoon olive oil

½ cup chopped onion

½ cup chopped celery (optional)

2 garlic cloves, minced

1 tablespoon curry powder

1 can (28 ounces) diced tomatoes

½ cup diced carrots

1 teaspoon ground cumin

⅛ teaspoon ground red pepper

2 cups chicken broth

¾ cup lentils

3½ cups fresh spinach chopped

Trim fat from lamb and cut into 1-inch cubes. Heat oil in Dutch oven over medium heat until hot. Add onion, celery, and garlic; sauté 2 minutes. Add lamb; sauté 5 minutes or until browned. Add curry, cumin, and pepper; stir well to coat. Add broth, lentils, and tomatoes; bring to a boil.

Reduce heat and simmer uncovered 20 minutes, stirring occasionally. Add spinach and carrots; simmer 10 minutes or until lamb is tender. Remove from heat and serve with bread and a green salad.

|||||||||||||||| DISCUSSION AND REFLECTION ||||||||||||||||||

1. If you were counseling a friend who was overly stressed, how would you use the story of the Bedouin shepherds to encourage and guide her?

2. What things are you involved in that create stress for you and your family? Do you believe that if you don't resolve these issues, they will be detrimental to your health? Your relationships? Your marriage? Explain.

3. What will it take for Americans and others in cities around the world to make a change? Are you willing to make changes, even if the rest of the people around you don't? What are some practical steps you can take?

4. Identify one personal action step you can take toward adopting a life of real simplicity.

The Circle of Life

Restructuring Our Relationships

The theme song of Disney's popular animated movie and Broadway play *The Lion King* is "Circle of Life." This song accurately depicts a beautiful way of life for the animal kingdom and a call to live in rhythm with the circles of life. There is the cycle of life and death, the cycle of the sunrise and the sunset, the cycle of the seasons. But there is another very important circle of life that deals with relationships and community. It's an axiom most Americans living in urban and suburban areas are unaware of and are violating to their detriment physically, emotionally, spiritually, and relationally.

Let me explain. Go to chapter 1 and find the diagram of the different worlds you and your family manage (page 23). It's not uncommon for a family of five to have thirty-plus different relationship groups to sustain. It doesn't take Dr. Phil to conclude that this pattern of life creates stress and discontentment. Consider for a moment that your drawing represents the life of someone who comes to you for advice on how to improve his or her situation. What would you say to them?

Most likely you would use action words like *prioritize*, *eliminate*, *simplify*, and *consolidate*. This simple advice would be right on track and rooted in wisdom. Social specialists use a different language to say the same thing. They tell us that we need to exchange a host of *linear contacts* for a circle of community. For example, American Institute of Stress physicians and sociologists tell us that it is possible to be in the company of others and still feel isolated. Why? Because many people have a large group of "friends," but in reality most of them are mere acquaintances.[1]

The Linear Model

What is the difference between linear contacts and a circle of community? Diagram the linear relationship theory, and it will likely resemble the drawing of your world. There is a relationship of some sort between you and another person (a *line* drawn to them), but they typically do not share a relationship with the other people in the other worlds you manage (they are not in the same *circle*).

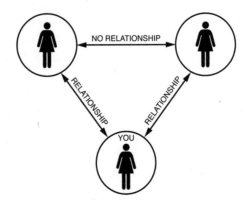

At first glance, this may not seem to be a serious problem. As a matter of fact, you may have some relationships that you would rather not expose to your preferred relationships. While this separation may spare you some embarrassment and frustration, in the long run this may not be what's best for you.

In a linear relational model, you run from one relational unit to another. You go to work; you call your father or sibling on the cell phone; you attend your son's soccer game; you meet with your financial adviser; you answer an e-mail from a former coworker; you go to church. As you exit one world and enter another, there may be some mention of the people you just left behind, but essentially they are not connected to the present world in any meaningful way.

To capture just how disconnected these worlds can be, imagine inviting just one person from each world you manage to your birthday party. You will go to bed that night utterly exhausted. Why? Because the only thing these people have in common is you. One of our friends recently did this and confessed that it was like keeping twenty separate plates spinning as she moved from room to room and person to person trying to keep everyone happy. She went to bed exhausted and wasn't sure she wanted to do that again the next year.

The most damaging aspect of linear friendships is that no one really knows the real you. This can even include your mate, as he or she is often out of the loop on significant relationships you manage. I'd like to offer this thought: *A person doesn't really know you unless they know most of the people in your other circles.* Why? Because the most important thing about you is the relationships you have—your relationship with God and your relationship with others. For community to be authentic and strong, people have to share in these relationships with you.

In linear worlds your mate may not know much about the people you work with day in and day out. The women in your Bible study group may never see you relating to your children. In linear friendships you lack a group of people who know the *whole you* (your dreams, fears, hopes, quirks, and history—your unfolding story). Each world knows bits and pieces but doesn't share the big picture. And it really isn't feasible that they can. Linear friendships have some merit, such as a greater degree of privacy, an ability to exit one relationship without seriously affecting the others, and less accountability. But the downside far outweighs the few temporary temptations and benefits. Two-thirds of all people who struggle with stress cite loneliness as their major problem, even though hundreds of people surround them each day.[2] As mentioned in chapter 1, this is called *crowded loneliness.* In the end, the linear world leaves us isolated, misunderstood, exhausted, anxious, and shallow.

The Circle of Relationships

In order to bring a deep sense of belonging to his or her life, the busy modern-day person needs a *circle of relationships*—a collection of people of all ages and stages who daily flow in and out of each other's lives. One of the secrets behind the success of this model of community is that the people know not only you but each other as well. It is an extended family of spiritual aunts, uncles, grandparents, nieces, and nephews who are committed to living out their faith in a simple, radical, and intentional way. This circle of friendships can also include those who don't live by faith in God but still share in the daily life experiences of a person. Together they share in the mundane exchanges of life: taking out the trash, checking the mail when the other person is out of town, sharing the rental fee on a rototiller, playing a game of kickball in the street, watching a classic movie together—the list goes on.

Take note of the simple illustration of a circle of friends. Instead of the complex milieu of isolated relationships, which promotes crowded loneliness, we have a simple circle of relationships where people interact

not only with you but also with each other. It is this approach to relationships that gives us the greatest chance of meeting the connection requirement discussed in chapter 2.

So much of the richness of life comes in the journey to the event, not in the event itself. Many of the experiences that make life sweet are the little nuggets that come our way when we least expect them. Read the gospels, and you'll discover that many of Jesus' meaningful conversations with the disciples took place between events. In Old Testament times, Moses instructed the Israelites that the most important lessons in life are best caught in the everyday movements of life rather than in formal events and classrooms.

> Hear, O Israel: The LORD our God, the LORD is one. Love the LORD your God with all your heart and with all your soul and with all your strength. These commandments that I give you today are to be on your hearts. Impress them on your children. Talk about them when you sit at home and when you walk along the road, when you lie down and when you get up. Tie them as symbols on your hands and bind them on your foreheads. Write them on the doorframes of your houses and on your gates.
>
> Deuteronomy 6:4–9

A major problem with linear friendships in suburban America is that the relational opportunities in the journey to another place are eliminated. Each individual, isolated in an automobile, makes his or her way to the event, and thus much is lost. The sayings of Solomon offer this wise counsel: "Do not go to your relative's house when disaster strikes you — better a neighbor nearby than a relative far away" (Proverbs 27:10). Loosely paraphrased, Solomon is saying, "If you're having trouble and you have to get in a car to find help, you're in more trouble than you know."

This is the vision presented in *The Connecting Church*, which recommends that we move beyond commuting to small group events in search of "contrived community" to living in a circle of relationships with the people nearby—the place where community can truly happen.[3] How is this possible given the hectic lives we live? The counsel at the beginning of the chapter is here applied. We prioritize, consolidate, eliminate, and simplify the linear worlds we have to the best of our ability, to the measure of our faith, and to the quota of our courage in order to create a circle of life. Paul Rosch of the American Institute of Stress drives home the importance of this concept by posing the question, "How many friends do you have?" Here are his thoughts:

> Before the agricultural revolution, isolated settlements probably consisted of about 100 people. Since these individuals probably had fairly close daily interactions, varying degrees of friendship probably developed among almost all of them. Interestingly, some authorities feel that 100 people is close to the maximum number of true friendships one can ever expect to develop in a lifetime. Today, some city dwellers may come into contact with up to 1,000 people in just one day. Many high schools in large cities have 5,000 students, or 50 times more people than our ancestors would have ever encountered in a lifetime! Sadly, although there are many more opportunities for establishing friendships today, it is equally apparent that less time is available to nurture them.[4]

Today we are overstimulated with people exposure, which affords us surface contact at best. This has many negative effects on our lives, including some of today's modern disorders and phobias. Because we are inundated with the sight of people and sound-bite contacts, we often don't see clearly that we need deep encounters with only a hundred people or less. Consider the average stop to get a tank filled with gas. You may see upwards of ten people and have zero contact with any of them as you dip your credit card into the machine and get on with your business.

Therapist Will Miller observes, "If you talk to any therapist today, the problems we see mostly are mood disorders: depression, anxiety, loneliness, and social detachment. As blessed as we are as Americans, as prosperous as we are, there's all this depression. So where is it coming from? I'm convinced it's rooted in the loss of 'refrigerator rights' relationships."[5] This is a delightfully clever way of describing a different kind of relationship. A person with refrigerator rights is someone who can come into our home and feel comfortable going to our refrigerator to make a sandwich without our permission. Miller argues that too many Americans suffer mentally and emotionally because they have too few of these kinds of relationships.[6]

One of the major causes of a milieu of surface relationships and absence of deep relationships is mobility. Every year, approximately 17 percent of the entire American population moves away from the people they know or are beginning to get to know—and it's been going on at this rate for close to twenty years now.[7] The mobility is often driven by the prospect of a more promising career or the desire for higher wages. Most people give little thought to the overall effect of these moves on their family's physical, emotional, and spiritual health. This game of musical careers is a key reason for the dominance of the linear relational model that is so debilitating.

The challenge is to find the "center place" that allows you to integrate as many relationships and activities as possible into a circle. Is there a way to bring the worlds of work, school, family, recreation, and church into one circle? For the Christian, is there a place where you can bring into one circle your relationships with believers in Christ and your relationships with those who don't believe?

While adopting this model of relationships may seem impossible or even a little "Mayberryish,"[8] it is the pressing issue to address. We cannot continue to deny that we were created for community and that the present-day linear structure is not meeting the requirements. It is pseudo-community, not real community. We must connect the dots between our lack of community and our declining health. Harvard Medical School professor Jacqueline Olds makes this pertinent observation:

America is in the midst of a loneliness epidemic—and the isolation is undermining our health ... Our seeming obsession with the most intimate details of strangers' lives—as evidenced by the rise of "tell-all" television talk shows—is another manifestation of our isolation. When you lack a circle of people you know well, gossiping about strangers is a way to fill the gap. But it isn't very interesting.[9]

After years of searching full-time for the holy grail of community, I have found nothing as compelling as the neighborhood. Neighbor-

In the 1950s, suburban shopping malls were coming to the landscape of modern America. Prior to this time, shopping was done in small Ma and Pa shops built in centers of towns, close to the street, with sidewalks for pedestrians to walk between them. Most of the stores were in urban settings. As an independent grocer, my father was part of that setting.

For my family in Cleveland, Ohio, our shopping megaproject opened in 1966, about the time I was seven. Curious about this new shopping extravaganza, my family headed to the Richmond Mall one Sunday afternoon after church.

As I remember it, we passed up our normal Sunday lunch of pasta with Mom's homemade sauce to experience lunch in a dime store called Woolworth. Then we meandered through the main avenues of the mall, exploring all the stores under that one huge roof. My parents looked at appliances, and I was bored. Feeling comfortable in this superstore setting, I strolled off into the next department, where the pretty dresses were calling my name. I was exercising my innate female desire to shop. After a few moments of looking at dresses, I turned around, only to realize that my family wasn't where I thought they'd be. In fact, they were nowhere in sight. Panicked but trying to maintain a calm exterior, I wandered around trying to find them, and I discovered the exit of JC Penney opening into the vast corridors of the mall. I don't remember much after that, except that I was looking around anxiously at the sea

hood or place-based community allows us to draw the greatest number of people into a circle—our spouse, children, other Christians, those who don't believe in or follow Jesus, older people, younger people, recreational or affinity friendships (golfing, vacation interests, hunting, reading groups, dog show enthusiasts, for example), and school friends. With a little intentionality it can also contain most of the activities we currently commute to—small groups, recreation, car pools, compassion projects to help the needy, and so on. Most important, neighborhood

of faces to see if I could find a recognizable one. None of them were my family members, yet there were hundreds of faces, all towering above my three and a half foot head.

This describes "crowded loneliness" to a tee. All I wanted was to see someone who knew my name. Finally, after what seemed an eternity, I heard not my name but my nickname, Corkie, in a muffled yell from the familiar voice that had dubbed me with that title a few years earlier. An instant calm came over my body as I looked up and saw that person who not only knew me well enough to know my name but even knew my nickname. It was my dad, calling out from the second story where he and my brother had climbed to see if they could spot me. Not too long after this, my mother's warm arms embraced me lovingly as she scolded, "Don't ever scare us like that again!" Sorry, Mom and Dad!

We are raising a generation that never knew a time when there weren't shopping malls—a generation that thinks relationships are just a slew of acquaintances from Facebook. We must get back to a place where people not only know our names but our nicknames, or perhaps know us well enough to give us a nickname. How can we do this and keep all of the relationships intact? Keep reading. Randy and I delight in unfolding our journey into simplifying our relational worlds into a life of true community.

Rozanne

community enables us to park our cars and to see people between events as we engage in our everyday activities. It is in these frequent and spontaneous encounters that so much of the richness of life is experienced. Apart from the neighborhood, these kinds of experiences are simply not available to us today without planning ahead.

The power of place-based community is that it creates the most tangible circle of relationships—the place where everyone of various ages and backgrounds knows you and can also know each other. While the neighborhood structures in suburbia are a far cry from those functioning for centuries in small villages around the world, which also included workplaces and marketplaces within that circle, it's still the best center place I know of for facilitating community.

When World War II ended, Massachusetts Institute of Technology converted former military barracks into tiny apartments for the ex-servicemen who attended the university. At the time, researchers Leon Festinger, Stanley Schachter, and Kurt Back were studying attraction and liking, and they saw these apartments as a kind of laboratory in which to study friendship formation. After the students had been living in the apartments for a couple of months, the researchers asked them questions about how and with whom they had made friends, including certain things they might have in common, such as the branch of military they served in, their hobbies, their major in school, their hometown, and so on.

The researchers discovered that friendship wasn't based on any of these possible common attributes; rather, the biggest predictor was *proximity*—how close people lived to each other. Forty-one percent of the friends lived next door to each other, 22 percent lived two doors away, and only 10 percent of the friends lived on the opposite end of the floor. They called this finding "the proximity effect."[10]

This is not a new idea but one that has stood the test of time over the centuries. Those of us who live in the suburbs have lost our way through all the fascinating gadgets our minds and money have been able to create—things that have pulled us to and fro and isolated us from each other (suburban houses, select sports, the backyard oasis, automobiles, satellite television, air conditioning, and on and on it goes). But there are signs that this is changing. According to the Trends Research Institute in Rochester, New York, Americans are starting to "de-cocoon"—to come out of the self-sufficient homes they built in the suburbs and return to a connected life.[11]

Let's see if this could work for you. Take a sheet of paper and draw a single circle. Ideally, this circle would portray about a one-mile radius from your home. Now go back to your drawing in chapter 1 and see how many relationships and functions you can consolidate into this circle. At first it may seem impossible because you may not know anyone in your neighborhood or apartment complex. But what if you did? What if you made a commitment to park the car and hang out at home? What if you were to decide to participate in your hobby with others in your neighborhood who had similar interests (golf, bowling, mechanics, cooking, dog shows, and so on)? What if your children concentrated on playing with kids in the neighborhood; after all, they probably already go to the same school? What if you worked it out to sign up for the same sports team? What if you carpooled to school and your kids' events? What if you invited empty nesters to your school's football game on an autumn Friday night? What if you had at least one meal a week with another family in the neighborhood?

How about a game night? What if you organized a simple night of pickup basketball every Thursday night in the neighborhood? What if you formed a small group with people in your neighborhood? What if your small group decided to reach out to the poor and needy around you —or visited the local nursing home once a month? What if you took a vacation or camping trip together? What if you planned a Fourth of July block party? What if you took walks through the neighborhood with those who were interested? What if you concentrated on sharing your faith with those neighbors you, your family, and other believers in your neighborhood were already connected to? What if you just enjoyed a simple conversation as you ran into each other as you took out the trash or retrieved the mail? The possibilities are endless.

Here is some good news: This is a description of a *circle of relationships*, and it meets the connection requirement and eliminates crowded loneliness. But you may be thinking, *I don't have time for this.* Don't be discouraged. The next chapter will lay out a simple vision for making time for relationships.

We must find our way back to the circle of relationships. Jesus said that you can't "pour new wine into old wineskins" (Matthew 9:17). But is it possible to pour old, vintage wine into new wineskins of the twenty-first century? I believe we not only can but *must!* So many highly successful people are like the Adam of old — encased in beautiful surroundings with no care in the world when it comes to material things but in deep trouble on the inside. They are suffering from isolation and loneliness. The superior design is to have a circle of friends in which people are connected not only to you but to each other as well. This garden of relationships provides a rich soil where roots can grow deep. If planted correctly, this principle of circular community can greatly simplify your life as well as add great meaning as each member takes in the communal oxygen God intended. The air of linear relationships is available — but toxic and harmful. It can give the sense that it is sustaining us relationally, but little by little we are being poisoned.

What are the practical steps to creating circles out of straight lines? I am excited about the words you will read in the following chapters. I offer you the hope of a "circle of life" to save you from crowded loneliness. In the words of a pig and a hyena from *The Lion King,* I wish for you *hakuna matata* ("no worries") — a reduction in stress and anxiety.

|||||||||||||||||| DISCUSSION AND REFLECTION ||||||||||||||||||

1. How many people have you granted "refrigerator rights" to in your life? Does this feel more like an invasion of privacy or an expression of intimacy to you?

2. What is the hardest thing you would face in consolidating your worlds?

3. What do you think of the suggestion that your neighborhood is the best "center place" for community? What would change positively or negatively if all the members of your small group lived within walking distance of each other?

4. Identify one personal action step you can take toward adopting a life of real simplicity.

The Hebrew Day Planner
Restructuring Our Time

OK, I'm sure at least some of you think we've lost our marbles by suggesting that connecting with your neighborhood is the best way to create community and at the same time find balance and margin. "Sit on my front porch? When would I have time to do that? Don't you remember all those worlds I'm managing? Oh, and by the way, I don't even know most of my neighbors."

But you're still reading so we must have piqued your interest. Hang with us as we unveil the next steps of how you can begin to have time, not only to sit on your porch in the evening with your neighbors, but to enjoy your family and all the other things you do even more as you embrace your new life of real simplicity.

The modern craze over the last twenty years or so had us keeping track of life with a day planner. With the rise of technology, we now have palm-sized smart phones, with access to the Internet and the availability of our calendar, contacts, the weather, and a slew of other things I'm not sure how we ever lived without. With these electronic devices we plan our lives away. We write down appointments and keep track of anniversaries and birthdays. With high-tech planning, we can put together many to-do lists, and whatever we don't get done will just scroll over to the next day and then the next until it is completed and marked off the list. The better, more intentional planning gurus even try to get us to schedule time and appointments in a way that achieves our personal goals.

I have a smart phone fully equipped with the newest version of the modern day planner, which hourly syncs with my computer to keep my life in line. I am never without it! If the beginning of wisdom is to call something by its right name, then I don't think the best name is a day planner. We might call it a 24/7 planner. Or better yet, we might call it a "chaos manager." Connecting the popularity of this type of technology with the discoveries we've made in the first four chapters, we might call the day planner an "almanac for managing linear worlds."

The day planner is a tool to help us manage our exit from one world of people and projects into another world of people and projects within the same day. For the average American, this tool can help manage the entry into and exit out of five or six relational galaxies. If you are a mom or dad with active children, the day planner not only seeks to get the right child in the right place at the right time with the right chauffeur; it also promises to keep you from leaving one stranded on an isolated relational island somewhere in town — how embarrassing would that be? Have you ever walked your son into basketball practice only to see his teammates running out of the gym and the coach, ball under his arm and clipboard in hand, exiting as you enter? I have. I still remember the look on my son's face as we discovered that we were an hour late for practice. Technology is only as good as the operator. I am still technologically challenged. Trust me, it was embarrassing!

If you want to live a healthier, longer, and more meaningful life, a day planner is not your solution. Throughout history, people have seen no use for it. It is hard to imagine a Bedouin shepherd's mom using a smart phone. But let's try.

"All right, family, as you go out into the fields to watch over the sheep, remember that I have dinner scheduled in my smart phone for 5:00 p.m. sharp tonight."

The teenage shepherd boy and son would retort, "Mom, why do you have to put that into that contraption? We have dinner every night at the same time. And we're always there, right on time!"

While we may and can use a day planner to aid us in managing life, what we first need in advanced and more educated cultures is something more basic. Most people today have a daily and weekly pattern that is unbalanced and not sustainable over the long haul. I suggested in previous chapters that if we continue to live this way, it may well kill us. Not only are we not satisfying the connection requirement God created in us, but I'd also be so bold as to suggest that the way we plan our lives is the first obstacle to meeting this requirement.

I want to recommend an ancient concept that may be new to you. I'm calling it "the Hebrew Day Planner." This concept is rooted in the creation theology of Genesis 1 and 2. It goes back to our design as humans by our Creator—his specs on how we should function. In these two chapters of Scripture we are given the basic architecture for living a connected life. The Hebrew people were totally tuned in to these principles. It was the first story to be shared with their children around the fire at night.

The basic premise of the Hebrew Day Planner is that we were designed by God on the sixth day of creation to function in harmony and rhythm with what he created on the first five days. On the very first day, God created light and darkness.

> And God said, "Let there be light," and there was light. God saw that the light was good, and he separated the light from the darkness. God called the light "day," and the darkness he called "night." And there was evening, and there was morning—the first day.
>
> Genesis 1:3–5

On the fourth day, God filled the night and day with objects that governed the time of the day, the beginning and end of seasons, and the yearly calendar—in other words, a divine Rolex watch.

> And God said, "Let there be lights in the vault of the sky to separate the day from the night, and let them serve as signs to mark sacred

times, and days and years, and let them be lights in the vault of the
sky to give light on the earth." And it was so. God made two great
lights—the greater light to govern the day and the lesser light to
govern the night. He also made the stars. God set them in the vault
of the sky to give light on the earth, to govern the day and the night,
and to separate light from darkness. And God saw that it was good.
And there was evening, and there was morning—the fourth day.

Genesis 1:14–19

On the sixth and final day of creation, God made humans (Genesis
1:26–27). Now let's connect the dots. Do you think we were designed
by God in any way to function in harmony with the creation? More spe-
cifically, do you think the *divine clock* of night and day has any bearing
on our lives? I believe the answer is an unequivocal yes. I also believe
the evidence reinforces this conclusion.

As we look at the pattern of the Hebrew day, we see that God's
people have taken their cues from creation theology. Looking at the
circle below we see that God has divided the twenty-four-hour day into
two parts—night and day.

For the ancient Hebrew, there is a divine plumb line that governs
the patterns of the day: 6:00 a.m. (dawn) and 6:00 p.m. (dusk). Oddly
enough, the day begins for a Hebrew person the "day before," or at 6:00
p.m. This is consistent with the way God referred to each day in Genesis 1. After describing each day's creative work, the author of Genesis
concluded the section with these words, "And there was *evening*, and

there was *morning*—the first [second, third, fourth, fifth, sixth] day" (Genesis 1:5, 8, 13, 19, 23, 31, emphasis added).

At first this may not seem like a big deal, but it says something about the priorities of God's chosen people that we fail to understand today. We'll come back to this later. For now let's focus on the principle that life for the Hebrew person transitioned on dawn and dusk.

There are essentially three major activities in each day that should be governed by night and day: *productivity, relationships,* and *sleep*. Because the work of the Hebrew was agrarian, productivity was accomplished during the hours of sunlight—6:00 a.m. to 6:00 p.m. At 6:00 p.m. the sun would set and darkness would begin to descend. From that point on, the time would be devoted to relationships—time with family, extended family, and friends; sharing a meal; and a time of storytelling (no TV or Internet). This is where a Hebrew child would hear the creation story told over and over again. There would be no rush, because there was no place to go (no mobility). Between 9:00 p.m. and 10:00 p.m. everyone would settle down to get a good night's sleep. The basic structure of a normal day for the Hebrews went like this: twelve hours available for productivity and work (6:00 a.m. to 6:00 p.m.); four hours available for relationships (6:00 p.m. to 10:00 p.m.); and eight hours available for sleep (10:00 p.m. to 6:00 a.m.). The illustration below describes this basic structure.

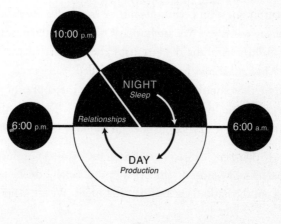

Each member of the Hebrew family would operate within these guidelines each day for six days (Sunday through Friday). On Friday at 6:00 p.m., the beginning of the seventh day, they would rest from their work (see Exodus 20:8 – 11, keeping the Sabbath day holy) in response to God's example.

> Thus the heavens and the earth were completed in all their vast array.
>
> By the seventh day God had finished the work he had been doing; *so on the seventh day he rested from all his work.* Then God blessed the seventh day and made it holy, because on it he rested from all the work of creating that he had done.
>
> Genesis 2:1 – 3, emphasis added

God again reveals a key design requirement of the human model. We function at peak performance when we take one day a week to rest and replenish. If we violate this design, we are abusing our bodies and souls, and little by little we diminish our effectiveness. So important was this principle for living that God modeled it by taking the seventh day for rest. Did God do this because he was tired? Does divinity perspire? I don't think so. God did not come to nightfall on the sixth day and say, "Thank me it's Friday." God is reinforcing a pattern that is essential for healthy, productive living.

The central question is this: *Should we live by the same divine clock?* I think the answer is yes! We are humans born from the original design model of Adam. Archibald Hart uses the wonderful example of a machine. Most machines have a recommended "duty cycle" or recommended time they should be in service during the course of the day in order to run optimally. He poses this question: "What is the human body's duty cycle?" And then he goes on to make this observation:

> I am sure that people differ here, but in my opinion our duty cycle is 50 percent, like most machines. Why do I believe this? The clues come from the natural cycle of day and night. We are supposed to

work during the day and rest at night. What has messed up this cycle is the invention of the electric light bulb. Now our bodies no longer have a sense of daily rhythm—unless we give it to them.[1]

This is not a newfangled idea. It is rooted in the way life naturally functioned for thousands of years. Writing about "the next society," Peter Drucker suggests that we will have to learn how to live in the places we've created for ourselves. He observes what we know all too well: "The twentieth century saw the rapid decline of the sector that has dominated society for ten thousand years: agriculture."[2]

We are living at the beginning of a huge shift with regard to human existence, and it isn't all good. The agricultural lifestyle of the last ten thousand years naturally flowed right in sync with the Hebrew Day Planner. The farmer would wake up in the morning in time to see the sunrise. He and his family would work during the precious hours of daylight. However, when the sun went down, the work in the field came to an end. With the animals comfortably stationed in their stalls or in the field, the farming family would enjoy an evening with a large, whole-food type of meal and good conversation, which is something people were much better at when television didn't exist. With the rise of radio they might enjoy an hour of storytelling or even a professional baseball game called over the airwaves. Everyone gathered in one room since the crazy idea of two or three living areas hadn't yet evolved. No one left the home in the evening to work out at the gym. During the daylight hours the farm provided all the aerobic exercise and muscle toning anyone could need. When it came time for bed, everyone slept well. It is the way life went for most people up until the twentieth century. Even in 1913, farm products accounted for 70 percent of world trade; today it accounts for only 17 percent.[3] As Dorothy Gale said in *The Wizard of Oz*, "Toto, I have a feeling we're not in Kansas anymore."

While there is nothing inherently or morally wrong with the shift from agriculture to industry to technology, there is something seriously at risk. In chapter 3, we discovered that poor Bedouin shepherds generally live longer than the average American. Their lives represent the simplest lifestyle of the agrarian society. This lifestyle flows most naturally with the creation theology of Genesis 1 or, as I'm calling it, the Hebrew Day Planner.

The lives we've created for ourselves (or were involuntarily born into) do not naturally have these boundaries built into them. Because we are new at this frantic way of life—just the last hundred or so years—we

When our family moved from Texas to Illinois, we began to experience a cycle we hadn't noticed while living in the Dallas/Fort Worth area. The more drastic change of the seasons was hard to get used to, and we struggled to adjust not only to the intense cold of winter but to the extreme shortness of the days as well. Somewhere in our twenty-two years of living in Texas we lost the sense of the need to embrace the seasons and flow with them as well as with the daily and weekly clocks God designed for us. In Chicago, where we were on the cusp of two time zones, it got dark around 4:30 p.m. in December and January—about an hour earlier than it did in Texas. As soon as the sun was down I felt weary. After dinner I felt as though it was time to head to bed, even though it was only about 7:30. I began to feel as though the animals had it right by going into hibernation, while we humans just keep going and going. I didn't want to go anywhere—it was too cold and dark

Randy and I began to notice that we were consistently getting tired earlier in the evenings as darkness descended, and we felt better if we just went with how we were feeling. We stayed in more, and some nights we wanted to go to bed at 9:00 p.m. Could it be that our bodies were divinely created to get more sleep in the winter and less in the summer? Randy and I believe this is true, and we've since added to our divine clock theory the divine calendar theory. As we've learned more about the way God created us, we believe God intended people to work in conjunction with the systems that he designed in nature. In agrarian don't have a good grasp on the overall impact it has on us as individuals. Significant results are now in, and there are, to be sure, many exciting aspects of living in a global society with unprecedented technological inventions. The rise of these inventions most brilliantly manifests the reality that we who are created in the image of God have an amazing ability to create. I am still blown away when I talk to my father in Cleveland, Ohio, in real time, using a tiny little wireless contraption

cultures, this happens naturally. Planting, plowing, and harvesting happen during the seasons when the days are longest. The ground is dormant during the winter months — a time for replenishing for the earth and the people.

During our three years in a Chicago suburb, our family often found ourselves in our basement family room, wrapped in blankets, watching our favorite TV programs or a movie. This room became our favorite spot in the house and created the fondest memories of our time in the Windy City.

At one point, one of our neighbors was having their kitchen remodeled, and they found it challenging to use the little microwave and hot plate for cooking, so we began inviting them over. Almost every Monday night they joined us to share a meal and to watch the TV series 24 together. Finally the kitchen work was finished, but the program wasn't, and so we kept getting together. Our lifestyle changed with the seasons. In the summer we played outside with neighbors; in the winters we were tucked inside our cozy little basement with neighbors. See a pattern here? Now back in Texas, we enjoy doing the same thing. We work hard all day, but at night, as dusk settles over our house, you'll likely find us having dinner around our dining room table and then nestling in for an evening of watching HGTV (Home and Garden television network), viewing a movie, playing games, or just visiting with neighbors.

Rozanne

called a cell phone while I am visiting someone in California. This is a beautiful thing—and something to be celebrated.

However, we haven't been careful to monitor the effect these changes have on our need for community and balance. We live in a world that does not require boundaries. Night and day have been made nonissues in our 24/7 halogen bulb society. I can recall numerous occasions when I took my children to a professional baseball game during the last few hours of daylight. At about the seventh-inning stretch I looked up in the sky and realized that somewhere along the line it had become night, but I had missed it. With seamless precision the major-league-wattage lights came on and drowned out the darkness. As far as I was concerned, it was still daylight. While we can celebrate humanity's creative genius

You may have decided that we've have lost our minds. The Hebrew Day Planner is certainly not compatible with the way most of us lead our lives in the twenty-first century. But you must admit that you probably don't get enough rest. Did you know that 83 percent of people between the ages of eighteen and twenty-nine sleep with their cell phones?[4] If e-mails aren't returned the same day, or sometimes the same hour for our more demanding contacts, someone isn't happy. So we stay up late because we can, making sure we stay on top of every demand.

As a mom, another side effect of our constant workload concerns me. When I was a kid, I used to stay home when I didn't feel well. Does anyone stay home anymore when he or she is sick? We just keep on going—sharing our symptoms with the rest of our classmates or office colleagues or friends. Even if we do stay at home, with our laptops, Internet, cell phones, and iPads, we don't get true rest even then. My point is that we're simply not getting enough rest to keep us healthy. Now I'm not suggesting you stay home from school or work on a whim, but when did we lose respect for keeping those nasty germs at home and giving our bodies time to heal?

Rozanne

(still infinitely short of divine power, however), we must recognize that we've done all this with little regard for the connection requirement discussed in chapter 2. This way of life may be wonderful in many ancillary ways, but it is killing us in the most basic of ways. We must wake up to this and make some serious adjustments.

I'm not suggesting we all become farmers. Surely this wouldn't suit me well, given my childhood experience in industry-rich Cleveland, Ohio. I would be at a great disadvantage to provide for my family in a farmers' world, given my uncalloused hands and two theological degrees. I hardly know how to buy fruits and vegetables at the grocery store, let alone how to grow them from seeds. I know how to wring my hands from stress, but I don't have the stomach to wring the neck of a chicken in order to eat dinner tonight.

However, I am suggesting that we rediscover the beauty of the Hebrew Day Planner as a timeless principle for a healthy life and that we go on to engineer our lives in such a way that we readapt to its role in our lives. This is the divine plan established at creation to give us the room we need to live healthy, balanced lives. This, I think, is one of our most pressing issues. If we don't address it, we must not expect to ever truly live the life God intended us to experience.

Now take a deep breath and put the book down. Think about your life for a few moments. Think about how this divine plan might be achieved in your life. Then pick up the book again and read on, as I share my thoughts on how we can accomplish this in our lives today.

Be sure to check out the Hebrew Day Planner Sample on pages 212–13. This is too important to ignore!

Pick one night this week and plan a family dinner. If you are single or married without children, invite a neighbor or neighbor family to enjoy a meal with you. I encourage you to take your first step toward working with the divine clock in your body. Having a neighbor or friends over means you likely won't go back to work. Make the evening casual and comfortable. Tell them to come comfortably dressed to share dinner and just hang out and visit, gather around the television to watch a movie together, or go out in the yard and play a game of beanbag toss. Your meal doesn't have to be fancy. Cook hamburgers or chicken on the grill and make a green salad. If you want to be adventuresome, try the Polish Boys I mentioned in chapter 3 (see the simple recipe below; adapted from the recipe for Polish Boys at Hot Sauce Williams, Cleveland, Ohio).

Mom Frazee's Polish Boys

4 *kielbasa sausage cut in half to make 8 sausages (use turkey summer sausage for a healthier twist)*

8 *hoagie rolls with a crisp crust*

1 *bag of shredded coleslaw*

1 *jar of Marzetti slaw dressing (or make your own)*

1 *bottle of Open Pit Barbecue Sauce (We like the spiciness of this sauce, but your favorite sauce will work great.)*

1 *bag of frozen French fries*

Cook French fries in oven (Mom Frazee deep-fried them) according to package directions. Cook kielbasa on the grill until heated through. While sausages are cooking, cut hoagie rolls (not all the way through) and put them aside. Put the coleslaw in a bowl and add the dressing. Put the barbecue sauce in a bowl and heat in microwave for a minute or so until warm.

When everything is done cooking, have everyone gather around the table and make their own sandwich. Open a roll and put some coleslaw on it. Then add some French fries on top of the coleslaw (yes, on the sandwich!). Put kielbasa on the bun and add barbecue sauce on top.

Yield: *8 servings*

Buon appetito!

Rozanne

|||||||||||||||||| DISCUSSION AND REFLECTION ||||||||||||||||||||

1. How does your family keep activities coordinated and schedules running smoothly? What kinds of tools do you use to help (for example, a combined calendar posted somewhere in the house for all to see, smart phones, weekly meetings)?

2. Do you believe we were created to conform to the divine clocks of night and day and the four seasons? Why or why not?

3. How does your current schedule compare with the Hebrew Day Planner? What changes or adjustments could you realistically make quickly so you could come closer to experiencing this simpler life?

4. Identify one personal action step you can take toward adopting a life of real simplicity.

PART 3

THE OBSTACLES

*Overcoming Bad Habits and Myths
about Raising Children*

Getting Life Out of Balance
The Need for Boundaries

In the last few years, I've taken up golf. I successfully avoided it for the first forty years of my life. My dad, an avid hunter and fisherman, always questioned the logic behind hitting a little ball and then chasing it, only to hit it and chase it again. He always said, "If you never hit it, you'd never have to chase it." But one day at a retreat I was compelled by my staff to join in a round of golf for the sake of team building. I didn't like the idea of playing a game I couldn't win, but I couldn't deny that team building was essential—so I went.

Things went pretty much like I thought they would—lousy! I even stopped keeping score. However, there was one swing of the club when everything came together for me (sadly, without my knowledge of what it was so I could reproduce it), and the ball just clipped off the club effortlessly and sailed high and long.

I've been hooked ever since. What I learned about that one success-ful swing, as I've tried over the last several years to make it more of a routine occurrence instead of a complete accident, is that golf requires two major things to come together in order to hit the ball right: You must do the *right thing* at the *right time*. Golf requires perfect align-ment, a proper grip, a good takeaway and backswing, and a good for-ward motion and finish (the right thing); *and* it must all be done with a flawless tempo or rhythm (the right time). So it is with life. We must not only do the right thing but also learn to do it at the right time and with the right tempo—in rhythm with God's divine plan. To quote a wise simile from golf guru Bagger Vance (played by Will Smith in *The Legend of Bagger Vance*), "The rhythm of golf is like the rhythm of life."[1]

This sense of rhythm is not taught by many people. As we discovered in the last chapter, people for the last ten thousand years didn't think much about it. The life of the shepherd and farmer had built-in boundaries that kept activities and the lack of activity in proper tempo. So when the pattern of life changed during the industrial revolution and now the technological age, no one had a clue about how it would affect our tempo of life or our ability to do the right thing at the right time. Those who did have a hunch were ignored by the masses.

One of the most common mistakes in a golf swing is to bring the

---

In order to lead a balanced life, you must have margin. Margin is time allowed for relaxation and replenishment; for enjoying relationships, dinners around the table, and hobbies; for thinking. It also allows for flexibility when the unexpected happens. But most of us live today with no margin left. Every moment is filled with activity and movement, and we even cut into our sleep time to get "stuff" done. Who hasn't wished there were a few more hours in the day?

When both parents work full-time jobs outside the home, it can lead to an eroding of our margin. This major development in our country's history has created what experts call the "work-family conflict," eating up most of the rhythm and tempo we once had. Women first entered the workforce during World War II, filling jobs previously carried out by men who had gone to serve our country. These women stepped up with a sense of excellence that proved women were as capable of working and supporting their families as men. They were the safety net of not only club down too fast. There is a false sense that the harder you swing the farther the ball will go. Nothing could be further from the truth. The downward swing of the club must be slow and in tempo with the rest of your body. When this happens, the ball goes effortlessly down the fairway. Archibald Hart makes this wise observation:

> Humans were designed for camel travel, but most people are now acting like supersonic jets. In a nutshell, most of us are living at too fast a pace.... The pace of modern life is stretching all of us beyond our limits. And we are paying for this abuse in the hard and painful currency of stress and anxiety—plain and simple.[2]

Most people believe that if we increase our speed, we will live happier and longer lives. This is simply not true. We must live our lives in tempo. This doesn't mean, however, that you'll get less done. Just as a

their families but our country as well. When the men returned home, most of those women returned to their homes and families as well. However, during the 1970s many women who previously would have been stay-at-home moms entered the workforce in order to give their family an economic edge or in response to the feminist movement.

While I have nothing against women or mothers working, many of my close friends do (I believe that the Proverbs 31 woman worked to bring an income to her family). I do want to point out that when both parents work, it lessens the margin for time the family has to spend together and causes everyone to be a bit more tired because there is less time to rest and replenish. Sabbath and evenings are spent doing laundry, ironing, housekeeping, and yard work. We have seen the most success in two-income families when one or both of the parents has flexibility in their schedules to satisfy the demands of the family.

Rozanne

rhythmic golf swing propels a golf ball, we can ultimately get further with a balanced life.

In the last chapter we discussed three major movements in the average person's day: *work*, or productivity; *relationship* time; and time for *sleep*. If we are to live simply, we must balance these three areas according to the tempo God created. However, most Americans live life out of balance in these three areas.

Work Imbalance

The Bible tells us that work is good and right. At creation, God gave men and women work to do with regard to managing his creation (Genesis 1:26). Solomon tells us that God gave us work to do and that we should enjoy it as a gift from God (Ecclesiastes 5:19). As a matter of fact, the Bible clearly states that the person who does not work should not eat (2 Thessalonians 3:10). The principles of the proverbs repeatedly proclaim that laziness is unacceptable and can only lead to poverty and impending doom (Proverbs 6:9–11; 19:15; 20:13).

However, God has set clear boundaries on our work. The Bible tells us (Genesis 2:2–3; Exodus 20:8–11; 23:12) that we should only work six straight days before we take a day for rest and replenishment. Jesus reminded us that we were not created for this principle, but that the principle was created for us (Mark 2:27). In other words, God created us with a duty cycle that requires us to be shut off one day a week. The Bible also tells us that too much work is not good. Solomon offers us these words of balance: "Better one handful with tranquillity than two handfuls with toil and chasing after the wind" (Ecclesiastes 4:6).

If work could be grabbed with our hands, we should seek to take only one fistful of work, and in the other we should grab a handful of tranquility. This is a fifty-fifty proposition. Fifty percent of our day should be given to work and productivity—this is good. Fifty percent of our day should be given to relationships and sleep—this is also good and necessary. It is a matter of balance.

You may be thinking, *I get all the relational time I need at work.* This seems to be a reasonable suggestion. Why can't we simply mix work with relationships and extend the time we work into the late hours of the night? For hard-driving individuals this appears to make sense. However, experts who study people who suffer from physical and emotional disorders suggest that the underlying source for their struggles is a lack of meaningful personal — as opposed to professional — relationships and support.[3]

For moms, the Hebrew Day Planner is even more difficult. After all there is a full-time job right here in our homes. The ironing, the laundry, the bill paying — and the list goes on. It is as easy for me to violate this principle as any attorney or business executive. "If I throw another load of laundry in after 6:00 p.m. it will only take a second," I rationalize. Then, of course, I need to fold it before I go to bed at 10:00. Or perhaps, I'll just empty the dishwasher so I don't have to do it in the morning when I wake up. Invariably I notice that my desk needs to be cleaned off before I head to bed — already thirty minutes behind my family — and if I sit down at my desk, it won't take me but a minute to answer just a couple of e-mails. Resting on the seventh day is even more difficult.

At first it was a struggle to not want to get a jump on tomorrow's to-do list. The single thing that helps me most in stopping my workday is to shut my computer off. Closing the laundry room door is also a help since I am an out-of-sight out-of-mind kind of person. Having friends for dinner is a great distraction because I can't go back to work while they are here. Knowing that my family is waiting for me to be with them after 6:00 p.m. is a wonderful restraint. If you want to implement this principle, try going public by publishing a book about it, and the stakes go up even more. Oops, my grandbaby girl just walked in, saying, "Nona?" So I'll be quitting now — and for sure I won't be back tonight!

Rozanne

Solomon tells the story of a wealthy man who is isolated and all alone. He has many possessions but can't seem to find peace with them. In a moment of dark despair, the man cries out, "For whom am I toiling,... and why am I depriving myself of enjoyment?" Solomon concludes, "This too is meaningless—a miserable business!" (Ecclesiastes 4:8).

It is common in America for work not to be properly balanced. It's not that all people work hard or efficiently when they are on the job. Probably very few do. However, many people don't do their work within the boundaries God has provided. It seems that this principle is violated most flagrantly by the highly "successful," highly driven type A personalities. This is the person many of us most want to become because he or she is the one who ends up with the most toys.

Accumulation is a full-fledged approach to life that is blindly addictive. Success is measured by how much you have accumulated compared to everyone else. It's how the game is played. Some call it "luxury fever." Solomon writes, "And I saw that all toil and all achievement spring from one person's envy of another. This too is meaningless, a chasing after the wind" (Ecclesiastes 4:4). Yet not too many paragraphs later he writes, "I have seen another evil under the sun, and it weighs heavily on mankind: God gives some people wealth, possessions and honor, so that they lack nothing their hearts desire, but God does not grant them the ability to enjoy them" (Ecclesiastes 6:1–2). Work is good—and even given to us as a gift from God—but when it is unbalanced with regard to the other necessities of life, something goes terribly wrong.

Work refers not merely to what we do at the office or factory. Work is activity and motion—yard work, exercise, children's sports, church meetings, and so on. In the previous chapter I suggested we should work from sunrise to sunset—from 6:00 a.m. to 6:00 p.m. We should work our little hearts out during this season of the day. But when dusk hits, we need to be done with our work for the day.

When we work is one major issue, but *where* we work is another matter to be addressed. With the rise of the automobile and the superhighway system, Americans have the capability to live in a suburban area

For our family, we've drawn a circle with a ten-mile radius around our house. We try to do all of our commuting, errands, and shopping within this radius. I see four major benefits to be gained from this exercise. First and foremost, it allows for more margin by reducing commute times and keeping me out of the car. Second, it is green; lowering the emissions created by long commutes is good for the environment. Third, when shopping locally, I am more likely to run into the same people again and again, which reduces the number of my relational worlds and deepens my relationships by giving me opportunities for countless mini-conversations with people who live near me. Fourth, it bolsters the economy of my own community.

Rozanne

—where only houses, convenience stores, and restaurants exist—and get up each morning facing a thirty- to sixty-minute commute to work. In some places in the Northeast and on the West Coast, the commutes can be up to ninety minutes each way. With the 8:30 a.m. to 6:00 p.m. workday being normative for many upwardly mobile people, one must leave the home at or before 7:00 a.m. and not get home until 7:00 or 7:30 each night. When we push the envelope beyond 6:00 p.m., our house can feel more like a hotel than a home. Hundreds of thousands of people each night find themselves in bumper-to-bumper traffic, thinking to themselves, *This is just the way the "good life" is.*

And this isn't the end of it. For the average family, most evenings include running around town in the automobile for a variety of reasons—grocery shopping, church activities, children's sports practices or games, eating out, and so on. Not only has this running around seriously eaten into the family mealtime; it has also extended our work and activity time beyond our duty cycle, thereby taking a toll on our physical, emotional, spiritual, and relational well-being. However, the negative effects are released only slowly so that most people never really connect the dots between their work imbalance and their unhappiness and unhealthiness.

Relationship Imbalance

Not only is our work life unbalanced, but we also experience a serious imbalance in our relationship time. We simply don't get enough quality time with a close-knit group of people to meet the connection requirement. As we've seen, when the connection requirement isn't met over a period of time, things begin to unravel in all areas of our lives.

One of the reasons our relationship quota is not met is that our work responsibilities and our commute to and from work rob us of relational time. The best time slot during which to center in and focus on relationships is from 6:00 p.m. to 10:00 p.m. So important was this time for the Hebrew family of yesteryear that they started their day with the evening hours. The average American family simply isn't home in the evenings anymore. By the time we've finished working, driving back home, carting children back and forth to their late-afternoon and evening events, shopping, or working out, there is no time left for a full meal and meaningful conversation. No longer are mealtimes events but something we slip in between, or mostly during, activities. Because many in today's families are on such different schedules, everyone must learn to fend for himself or herself.

We haven't been taught the long-term value of sharing a meal and conversation at dusk; most people, therefore, believe that shoving a high-calorie, processed fast-food item down our throats while riding in a seven-passenger vehicle accomplishes the same end. It doesn't. We were born with the need to unpack our day within a circle of people who know us and deeply care about us. When we exchange this kind of simple existence for a motion-obsessed existence—which takes lots of discretionary money to pull off—new evils and new illnesses are birthed in our homes and in our bodies. Simply put, when our relationship time is unbalanced, life doesn't work.

Sleep Imbalance

Solomon tells us that "the sleep of a laborer is sweet" (Ecclesiastes 5:12). In other words, a good, hard, and honest day of work aids us in the sleep process. However, if this labor negates quality relationship time with a circle of family and friends, our sleep is drastically affected over time.

Sleep disorders have hit the American culture in epidemic proportions. Psychologist Archibald Hart drew this conclusion at the end of the twentieth century:

> About half of all adult Americans cannot fall asleep at night. Forty-nine percent of American adults suffer some form of sleep-related problems such as insomnia. One in six American adults suffer from chronic insomnia.[4]

This problem is solved not by accumulation but by community. We can't solve the problem by purchasing the latest mattress used by NASA, goose-feathered pillows, silk sheets, down comforters, and mahogany poster beds. In the end, the problem is the way we live our lives when we're awake.

Why is our sleep negatively affected when we miss the relational portion of our day? I come back to the divine clock that was set at creation. God has established our bodies in such a way that when the sun comes up, our bodies are stimulated to work. When the sun goes down, our bodies seek a transition out of the pressures of the day — pressures that are, in proper proportions, good and healthy — and into preparations for an evening of replenishing rest. How we use this time between work and sleep is vitally important. If we press our bodies and minds to keep working and if we keep making ourselves overstimulated and stressed-out — especially through driving around town to various events and activities, we will not be prepared for sleep.

Because I find the work of Archibald Hart so helpful, I want to summarize his thoughts from chapter 14 of *The Anxiety Cure*.[5] The center of our brain contains a "clock" called the *pineal gland* that accurately controls the rhythm of the brain. This brain clock is also the storehouse for serotonin. Serotonin is a God-given chemical that is released with precision and is responsible for ensuring that our body's physiology feels contentment and joy during the day hours. Not surprisingly, it works on the twenty-four-hour cycle of light and darkness. At a certain time each day, the serotonin is converted to melatonin (now synthetically produced, interestingly enough, and sold as a sleep inducer), which sets us up for sleeping. At the onset of darkness—around 6:00 p.m.—the melatonin is released, setting us up for sleep. Melatonin is God's natural tranquilizer. At the onset of sunlight (6:00 a.m.), the melatonin is converted back to serotonin, preparing us for the day of work.

Whenever we artificially extend the daylight beyond God's creative design and bring the stress of labor or stimulated activity, which in turn releases the toxins of adrenaline, we neutralize the effects of the melatonin, thus creating a potential problem with regard to the quality of sleep. Hart writes, "High adrenaline, caused by overextension and stress, depletes the brain's natural tranquilizers and sets the stage for high anxiety."[6] If we continue to violate this brain clock cycle, it will cease to produce and release the required melatonin. We will then live in a constant state of inner stress and anxiety, which creates all sorts of problems and fears, including insomnia.

Many years ago, Sir Francis Bacon made this insightful comment: "He that will not apply new remedies must expect new evils."[7] Americans cannot continue to live an unbalanced life, knowingly or unknowingly showing a disdain for God's design. We must make changes based on God's design, or we'll suffer the short-term and long-term consequences. We must make room for the life God intended us to live, not only because we desire it but also because it is essential for our continued existence.

Lack of sleep is not only the *effect* of living in stress but also (in some cases) the *cause* that throws other areas of our lives out of whack. Lack of sleep ultimately creates health problems that affect our productivity. We strive to extend the hours of daylight and starve ourselves of wonderful relationship time so we can get more done, but in the end it reduces our productivity. Also, lack of sleep can destroy relationships because it creates an internal imbalance that makes us unhappy, irritable people. Adding stress and irritability on top of our already depleted relationships makes even more elusive the chances of renewing them and getting them back on track.

All this may seem like theory—with too distant an application to interest the instant-gratification bent of the typical American—until you personally experience the crash. It happened to me several years ago and has stirred my passion for balance in my life.

There have been very few days that I've failed to thank God for leading me to become a pastor. There are so many aspects that totally fit who I am—writing, speaking, helping people develop spiritually, and participating in building life-transforming biblical communities. In the not so distant past, I'd work all day, come home in the evening with a briefcase full of work, and retreat to a home office. I knew I needed—and wanted—to spend some time with my family, although I was at a loss as to what to do with them. Most nights at home together degenerated into watching television. Since each of us wanted to watch something different, three televisions often ran simultaneously. If at any time the family left to run an errand, I'd opt to stay home. As soon as they drove out of the driveway, I'd crack open the briefcase. I had already calculated what I was going to do. What's more, after all family members went to bed and I had a brief conversation with my wife, I'd shake off the cobwebs and convince myself to go back to work. Many nights I'd stay up until one or two in the morning—a time I reserved for creative thinking and writing projects. Being a minister can be confusing because I could rationalize that I was doing my work for God and that this work ethic pleased him.

However, when you take a strong passion for work and place no boundaries on it, something unexpected develops over time. I found myself unable to go to sleep. I'm not talking about going to sleep and then waking up and then going back to sleep again. I'm talking about never going to sleep. I had no answers as to why. I understood that people who were stressed-out and worried about their lives sometimes had trouble sleeping, but this wasn't the case for me. While my work has always been quite overwhelming—mostly because of my passion for excellence and my desire to bring things to completion—I hadn't been particularly worried or concerned.

It was then that I learned that a person can be stressed without being distressed. Stress, which depletes the natural brain tranquilizers, can be driven by an overextension of our passions and the things we love. I was available 24/7 to give myself to the things I was passionate about, and that became a problem. I don't think most of us truly know how much stress we continually live with, whether good stress or bad stress.

Each evening as bedtime approached, I would get nervous and begin to fret over the fact that I could not achieve the most basic activity in life—the nonactivity of sleep. I remember being wide-awake and strolling around in the house. *Surely I couldn't be the only one who was struggling in our family.* But I was. I would stand by the bedside of my youngest son as he enjoyed a deep sleep, and I'd say to myself, *How did he get better at this than me? When did I forget how to sleep?* I felt extremely incompetent.

The pain didn't stop there. Not only did I experience a decrease in productivity and a sense of distance with regard to the affairs of my family and friends, but internal fears and anxieties started to emerge —and they had no content or logic to them. Without question, this was the most alarming season of my life. I thought I was losing my mind.

After a month or so of insomnia, I went to the doctor. (In my mind, the fact that I put off going to the doctor sooner confirmed my manhood.) The doctor I was seeing at the time didn't know me—at least I didn't think he did. I was so embarrassed to tell a full-grown man that I couldn't sleep and was now scared to death. I certainly didn't want him to know that I was a pastor. I rehearsed my story a million times in my head. When the moment of confession came, I explained my situation and waited for the doctor to call in the men with the white jackets. He paused and then said, "When you add up the stress level that accompanies your job, caring for four kids, and your passion for excellence, it's not surprising this is happening to you."

"You know what I do?" I quipped back, hoping I had misheard him.

"You're the pastor of a large church in town. Most people know who you are." Oh, no, my cover was blown, but I did begin to feel that help might be on the way at last. My doctor told me that I was having sleep problems because of my lifestyle and that I needed to make changes. Jokingly, he said that if I moved to Borneo, I would sleep like a baby because the pace of life is much slower there. I jotted down in my mental notepad a reminder to check on one-way airfares to Borneo. He prescribed a sleep medication for the next forty-five days as I promised to undertake life-changing adjustments.

This marked the beginning of the journey of installing the Hebrew Day Planner (see chapter 5) into my life. I traveled this road not from intrigue but from necessity. Because a low-stress lifestyle isn't taught in common places of learning or in the home, I had to go searching, and as I searched, some of the pieces started to come together. I entered into the phase of *knowing that I did not know how to live a balanced, connected life.* As I came to this point, I experienced a rush of excitement and hope.

The process of installing the Hebrew Day Planner has been gradual but deliberate. One of the things I learned is that Americans haven't been taught to live within any of the creation boundaries. I've also learned that Americans have carved a track of achievement and adrenaline highs that promotes this harmful pattern of life. Not every person in America suffers from what I'm writing about. Those who suffer the most seem to be those who drive hard to achieve a certain status in life and work. This conclusion, established by specialists, begins to explain why many of the illnesses and diseases caused by stress are unique to Americans.

While I want to achieve all that God wants me to achieve, and I surely do want my life to count, I've come to realize that God has established boundaries we must adhere to—a rhythm, if you will, that keeps us healthy, happy, and productive. When this rhythm is ignored, our relationships suffer. Based on the connection requirement, it is the most essential component of being human. When we starve ourselves of the "air of community," we begin to see new problems emerge: sleep disorders, anxiety disorders, irrational phobias, arrested productivity, and strained relationships.

Simply put, the American way of life is choking connectivity to others right out of our lives. If things stay as they are, the way we model for our children our approach to life will be to their detriment. It is a way of life not taught with words in a classroom but caught as children live out a significant portion of their lives in the backseat of a van or SUV. In golf, the swing you take over and over again becomes a part of your muscle memory—your muscle performs the swing without conscious thought. By the way we live, we teach our children to establish either a bad swing or a good swing into their muscle-memory approach to life. (I'll deal with this in more detail in the next two chapters.) Once muscle memory is established, it takes a lot of work and concentration to change it. To remedy this social illness, we'll need to look beyond the medications and monetary investments marketed to us everywhere.

As for me, I've never slept better without medication, accomplished more, and enjoyed a more wonderful circle of relationships. While I have a ways to go, I strongly recommend that you install the Hebrew Day Planner into your life by virtue of the confidence I have in God's original design for us. You don't solve sleep problems by working on sleep but by balancing sleep time with work and relationships according to the brain clock given by God. I wish I could say the same thing about my golf game!

As we run hard, our bodies only last so long. It is our prayer that we have reached you before you hit your wall. For those of you who feel as though you've hit the wall already and are dealing with depression or sleep disorders, we want you to know that there is hope beyond medication. In the next several chapters, we will offer real-life solutions that can get you back into the natural rhythm and tempo for which you were created. Making changes is never easy, but the changes you make are well worth the effort. While they may save your marriage and family, they will for sure protect your sanity.

||||||||||||||||| DISCUSSION AND REFLECTION |||||||||||||||||||

1. One-half of adult Americans struggle with sleep. Do you? What about depression? If you struggle with it, what could be some of the reasons? Given what we know about the way we are created, could a possible cause be an imbalance of work and relationships?

2. Rate yourself on how well you are balancing work with other aspects of life. If you sense that your work is out of balance, is this an unusual season in your life, or is it quite common? What changes can you make immediately to positively benefit your future physical well-being and that of your family?

3. Identify one personal action step you can take toward adopting a life of real simplicity.

Childhood:
An Endangered Species
How Our Lifestyles Affect Our Children

Childhood is fast becoming an endangered species. Thankfully, some are beginning to recognize this and act before it is too late. *USA Today's* lead front-page story a number of years ago was an article titled "Harried Citizens Take a Night Off":

> No homework, no practice, no clarinet lessons. No math league, no soccer, no SAT sessions. No swim meet, no Scout meet, no learning to sing. None of their usual scheduled things! Not tonight anyway, not in this town known for affluent, competitive, accomplished parents and children.
>
> It took a committee of eighteen people seven months and six meetings to plan it, but Ridgewood—where the calculus tutorial runs into the orthodontist appointment, followed immediately by the strength-training class—is finally taking what heretofore only a blizzard could impose: a night off.
>
> The night had its genesis the year before, when harried mother of three Marcia Marra realized how overscheduled her family was. She formed a committee to discuss the problem, and it talked about programs and discussion groups.

We said, "Wait, we're working against ourselves," says the Rev. Douglas Fromm. "Let's plan a night where nothing is planned."

The idea caught on, particularly after September 11, when the village of about 30,000 lost 12 residents. From a hill, you could see the World Trade Center fall. "People began to think about what is really important," Fromm says.

School officials promised a homework amnesty. Sports teams canceled games and practices. Churches called off evening classes.

Family Night's success will be measured only by each participant. Marra says, "We don't even want quality time; we just want more down time."

This being Ridgewood, someone asked for a list of suggested activities, but that was rejected as too well planned. And everyone laughed when someone else asked whether there'd be a prize for the family that had the best night off together.

"I hope they do it several times a year," says Noreen Romano, a psychologist with two teenagers. "Of course," she adds, "they'll have to schedule it into the calendar."[1]

This is a classic and common description of American life. The stronger the economic advantage, as in Ridgewood, New Jersey, the more extreme the pace often is. As you read the testimony above, you see people running from one world of relationships and activities to another. Instead of centering down with a circle of family and neighbors during the relational season of the day, moms and dads are "dividing and conquering" in automobiles that cost more than the house my dad purchased in the 1970s. You will also note that when the entire town decided to take a night off from all the activity, some didn't know what to do. While we can see that what we're doing is not healthy, we often continue doing it because it is what we know.

Humans are creatures of habit. When the Hebrews gained freedom from the hard life of slavery in Egypt and made their way to a new life of freedom, dignity, and blessing, they grumbled and wanted to go back to Egypt (Numbers 14:3–4). They knew how to do slavery—and they wanted to go back to familiar circumstances. They didn't know how to do freedom. I'm suggesting that we don't either. We are slaves to schedules, accumulation, and automobiles. And this evening chaos is primarily driven by the children's activities. This is what I call "the juvenile suburban dance." Here's the primary question: *Is this what the children really want or need?*

I've been married to my high school sweetheart for over twenty-nine years. We have four children whom we love deeply. When we began our family, as committed Christian parents we desired to go against the grain of "throwaway families" and "latchkey kids" and really invest in them. We wanted to be more involved than we perceived the previous generation to have been. How does one tangibly fulfill this mission? In suburbia, the mission is to sign kids up for as many activities as possible so they'll be exposed to as many wonderful opportunities as possible in order to shape their self-esteem and future options. The theory preached to me by experienced parents of teenagers when our children were toddlers was to keep children busy and off the streets. If you don't keep your children busy with activities that you control, they will certainly resort to drugs and gangs. We embraced this advice, and by the time our first child reached four years of age, we were running neck and neck with the best of the families in Ridgewood.

The different motivations swimming in our heads — and in the heads of other parents as we sat on benches at sporting events together — had well-intentioned goals:

- *Children's activities are a way to teach your child socialization skills.* If children aren't involved in these activities, the argument goes, they will be outsiders socially, which will then get them connected to the wrong crowd and drastically lower their self-esteem — possibly the number one fear of parents today.

- *Organized activities develop our children in that particular area that will give them an edge later in life.* For example, get your child started in soccer when she's four so that she can learn the skills needed to give her an edge in high school. With suburban high schools now having a myriad of students, only the very best get to play. Maybe, just maybe, she will shine and secure a soccer scholarship to a leading university. We want our children to do well. We also know that if they're going to sustain the lifestyle we've provided, they will need to be competitive and discover their unique approach to success.

- *Enrolling our children in various activities costs money and demonstrates that we're willing to invest our financial resources in our child's development.* Money flows toward priorities. When we sign up our children for these activities, we are communicating and confirming our priorities. For example, if you sign up your child for in-line hockey, you have league fees; the cost of in-line skates (which typically last for one season); the cost of pads, helmet, and hockey sticks; the cost of trophies at season's end—no matter whether the kids won all of their games or none (in order to promote self-esteem regardless of performance); and the cost of the coach's gift (not nearly enough to pay him back for managing the expectations of the parents involved). And don't forget another cost often overlooked when signing up your child: the cost of meals. Because sporting events invariably take place during mealtimes, you need to factor in zipping by a fast-food drive-through window. By my conservative estimation and personal experience, it takes $350 per season per child to play in-line hockey. With the reality that most kids in suburbia are involved in three or four sports (most sports now have fall, spring, and summer leagues)—and usually some sort of nonsport activity (music lessons, cotillion, and so on)—it's not unrealistic for a family with four children to spend three thousand to ten thousand dollars a year on children's extracurricular activities alone—a figure not much lower than the annual salary level of those living in poverty in America. If you add select sports (a very expensive sports program that involves high commitment and travel), you'll pay somewhere between a thousand and three thousand dollars a year per child per sport. This kind of financial and time commitment allows us to believe we're serious about our children's well-being.

Here is the first of two questions to ponder: *Are parents engaged in this excessive activity each evening because it is what they want to do?* While most of the parents I know would say they enjoy watching their children perform on the field, in their honest moments they'd confess that the excessiveness is really a sacrifice for the sake of their children's development. If you have a son who plays baseball, for example, it's likely he will have three practices a week during the dinner hour and two games a week—five evenings each week for just one child participating in one sport. The trouble with children's baseball games is that they take longer than most other sports. If your child plays the first game, you get to the field at 5:30 p.m. and are done at 7:45 and home at 8:30, as long as you don't stop for dinner. If your child plays the second game, beginning around 8:00 (on a school night), you get there at 7:30 and are done at 10:00 and home by 10:45. It's hard to believe that any parent really enjoys this way of life after spending a long day at the office or shop. However, because of the commitment we have to our children and because there is no other alternative to accomplish our goals, we allow it.

Here is the second question: *Is this really what the children want?* While children love to play and certainly enjoy some level of organized sports, I can't help but think that things have gotten out of hand. I believe that children prefer more hanging-out time, more unstructured time, more time with their parents at dinner rather than having their parents sitting on bleachers at a ball field or in a gym. As I wrote this chapter, I watched my three boys play with three other boys (all different ages) in the snow in front of a friend's vacation home. Parents are not supervising or organizing the activity; the kids are making up the play as they go, according to ideas that occur to them. They've had a snowball fight, and they've built a snowman and a snow fort. I just confirmed with my wife that they were outside for three hours. When I ask children and even teens, their overwhelming vote is for open-ended, child-led, and unstructured time together.

The way that privileged suburban families are raising their children flows from a genuine love for their kids. Some of it may flow from the guilt of spending so many hours at work. Discretionary cash and two fully gassed vans or SUVs fund this strategy. While there are benefits derived and some memories gained, I propose that this strategy takes away more from our children than it gives them. If we ever hope to truly achieve a life of real simplicity, we need to rethink the way we're raising our children. If you believe this, won't you join us and the people of Ridgewood in making a change motivated by this same intense love for our kids?

Recently my mind traveled back a few years to a phone call I had made one morning to a wonderful friend of mine. Her kids were a bit older than ours, and I knew she would have the answer to my question: "When do you sign your kids up for soccer?" David, our oldest boy, was six at the time. Her well-intentioned answer floored me! "She said, "He's six — well, most kids have been playing since they were four." There it was again — that feeling of guilt associated with motherhood. Is there ever a way to do this job right the first time? I hung up the phone, put the kids in the car as fast as I could, and drove to the office of the soccer association. Apologizing to the woman behind the counter for failing to come when my child was four (as though she were the offended party), I embarrassingly accepted the application, filled it out, and left praying for a team to accept my son, who was way behind because his mother was not on top of things. That was the beginning — well, actually it was the end. The end of sleeping in on Saturdays, of family dinners during the week, of Sunday afternoon naps, of date nights for Randy and me, and of spring cleaning, for sure!

It wasn't until several springs later, when we had three boys in baseball and soccer and one daughter playing softball on a team coached by my husband (for which I did all the paperwork), that it occurred to us we probably couldn't keep this pace up for much longer. My life as a mother had boiled down to keeping up with how we were going to get everyone to the fields on time for either practices or games while keeping rosters, scores, and lineups. I found myself constantly rearranging schedules in my head, and my day planner never left my side. (Technology was not a part of my life back then.) If I lost my pen I was in trouble, but if I misplaced that day planner, I was sure life would come to a screeching halt for all of us. Looking back now, I wished I had lost it instead of my mind!

It was during one of the rare occasions when we were sitting on the bleachers at the same baseball game that Randy asked me if I was going to do any spring cleaning that year. I just about took his head off with my response — in an explosive whisper so no one could hear! "Spring cleaning? Are you crazy, man? When would I fit that in? When am I home? What do we care what our house looks like; we're never there!" (Do you think I was a little on edge?) I'm sure he didn't see this coming, or he never would have asked. But we were at a point where something had to be done. The stress it was placing on our family was unbelievable. If I had a nickel for every time I used the words "hurry up" to our kids during those seasons, we would be millionaires! Those very words spark stress in the most stable child, not to mention his mother!

To be a bit cliché, let me say that if we knew then what we know now, we would never have started down the sports road — at least not so early on in our children's development. If your children are under five, here's some food for thought before you embark on this journey. According to the Institute for the Study of Youth Sports at Michigan State University, 70 percent of kids will quit playing sports by age thirteen.[2] Surprised? We were too. Why are they quitting? Because it isn't fun anymore. They are burned out! About the time their bodies are physically ready and able to play athletically (middle school) and their minds are able to "get in the game," they are quitting.

Parents sometimes justify the money and time they spend on sports with the hope that little Johnny or Nicole will receive scholarship money for college. In reality, only about 2 percent of high school athletes are awarded college athletic scholarships. There is far more money available for academic scholarships than athletic scholarships.[3] I believe this negates the noblest reason parents involve their kids in sports in the first place.

For those of you who have already gotten caught up in your children's sports, there is hope that you can successfully trade this chaotic custom for a much simpler routine, even if it is achieved only one step at a time. It will take courage and intentionality to change the lifestyle to which your family has become accustomed. Standing up to coaches (some of the most intimidating people I've ever met) takes more courage sometimes than taking a hit on a football field. In the next chapters, we will offer practical steps on how to disengage from this life-sapping, overscheduled existence.

Rozanne

|||||||||||||| DISCUSSION AND REFLECTION ||||||||||||||||

1. What do you think about the residents of Ridgewood scheduling a night off? Can you envision this happening in your community? In your family? Reflect on some of the things you would do together if everyone had the night off.

2. Three motivations are presented for scheduling so much activity for our children: (1) to teach them socialization skills, (2) to give them an edge later in life, (3) to show them they are a priority as we invest our financial resources in them. Consider the schedules of your family and your motivations for activities. Which of these motivations is most compelling to you? How might you accomplish your purposes without embracing excessive activity?

3. Children's lives today are overscheduled. Is this what the children really want? Explain your thoughts. Is this what the parents really want? Explain your thoughts.

4. Identify one personal action step you can take toward adopting a life of real simplicity.

The Lost Art of Play

Seven Ways Our Children Are Losing

I grew up on the east side of downtown Cleveland, Ohio. We were a lower middle-class family. We had one car, which my father took to work. Our activities as children involved playing in our neighborhood. No other options were available. One of our favorite activities was playing army. We didn't have plastic guns or helmets, or even fatigues. Our guns were made of self-created carved branches. There were no pools in the backyard—and thus no fences or potential lawsuits. We would roam the neighborhood, hide in trees, and always argue that our imaginary bullet hit the enemy and that he should fall down and play dead.

Hours would fly by. The only thing that interrupted our play was dinner. When the sun began to settle we knew it was time to head home. All of our fathers were blue-collar union workers who worked up robust appetites during the day. Dinner was always served at the same time. Tardiness was unacceptable and was usually accompanied by loving parental punishment.

Today's equivalent is quite impressive. When a child has a birthday, he invites all of his friends from all over the area to his party held in a child-designed entertainment center usually called something like *Fun-Fest*. Each invited child receives a token (at a cost of five dollars) to play a round of laser tag. Laser tag blows the doors off any neighborhood army. Each child enters a dark room and is given a vest, which includes the target your opponent shoots at, and a high-tech laser gun. Teams are divided into two—all assigned by adult employees. For fifteen or twenty minutes you run around in a dark room and shoot at each other and at other objects in order to collect points. There is no debate or conflict over who shot whom—the laser computer system referees that part of the game. At the end of the round, each child receives an computer printout that gives the team and individual scores. WOW! As a child, if I were given the choice of playing neighborhood army on Dover Avenue or playing laser tag at FunFest, I would have chosen laser tag at FunFest hands down! At least I would have the first dozen times. After that I think I might have opted for neighborhood army. I know my father would have.

Seven Deadly Sins

The way we are raising our children in stereotypical suburbia is taking its toll as we commit at least seven deadly sins against them. Dragging our children away from home in the late afternoon and evening hours to transport them to adult-driven, highly structured, age-graded activities has these negative effects.

Lost Creativity

Because adults organize most of these activities, children have lost the art of play or creativity in play. If a child has been raised with overextended and structured evening activities, they are ill equipped to know what to do if free time comes along. Because we buy houses today that store our stuff, and not homes nestled in street-friendly neighborhoods, many of our kids can't go outside and expect to play with kids in the neighborhood. In America it's likely that the majority of us don't know our neighbors well enough to feel comfortable with our kids playing with the neighbor kids. So our children retreat to their rooms and watch television or play video games. Parents know this isn't a good thing, so they just keep doing what their discretionary money allows them to do. The result? Kids today are not as creative as kids in previous generations.

Lost Leadership Skills

Jill Steinberg, associate specialist in child development at the University of Wisconsin–Madison, writes the following:

> A lot of the activities that kids have access to are very highly structured and not structured by kids themselves, but by adults, or the rules of the game. Normally, kids run games themselves if they are allowed to. But we've got them in structured day care and structured school settings. So they really have few opportunities to manage their activities on their own. But these are important experiences. By directing the activity, you learn how to negotiate rules. You learn to referee yourself. You learn how to take control and exercise leadership.[1]

The intent of today's style of suburban parental involvement is to show commitment, but we've forgotten to factor in the reality that our strategy would rob our children of leadership development.

Lost Mentoring

I grew up with a brother who is five years older than me. While there were a few times I threw things at him for picking on me, I looked up to him. When the kids in the neighborhood organized pickup baseball games in the parking lot of the farmers' market, my brother was usually a captain because he was older. As I remember, he always made sure I was picked for a team, even though I had little to offer. I watched him, mimicked him, and simply wanted to be like him. Because baseball requires a bunch of kids, our teams included kids of all ages. This kid-led, multi-grade play created all kinds of opportunities for mentoring. While it's true that not everything we saw was the right or the best thing, for the most part the experience was positive. (The same is true in the adult world of mentoring.) If something got out of hand, word quickly got back to the network of parents, and action was taken and the fear of God instilled—at least at my house.

I remember my mom commenting that she knew all of her neighbors because her kids were out playing with the kids who lived on our street. With our rear- and side-entry attached garages and busy schedules today, knowing our neighbors is, for many, a thing of the past. Many of our kids no longer attend schools with their neighbor kids because of a trend toward private schools and organized children's sports. As mentioned earlier, it takes long commutes to get our kids together with their friends, and we have less time to relax and enjoy our homes, yards, and neighbors.

If we can cut down on the time we spend away from home, particularly in the evenings, we can make our neighborhoods friendlier and safer. And if we can create safer neighborhoods, suddenly more desirable homes for people who want a safe environment become available in even lower-cost neighborhoods, helping to eliminate (or at least reduce) the need for couples to extend themselves beyond their means. The Neighborhood Watch program, heralded by most police departments, is based on the fact that neighborhoods will be safer if people know their neighbors well enough to sense when something out of the ordinary is happening at the homes around where they live. And it works to the tune of cutting crime in a neighborhood up to 40 percent.[2]

Steve Bankes took the idea of knowing his neighbors a step further and reaped more benefits than just reducing crime. Wanting a place to sit and watch his kids play (in the front yard), he has influenced his little corner of Oak Park (in the Chicago area) and is helping to transform the world. Along with two wrought-iron chairs, a table, and some snacks, Steve took his outgoing personality into his front yard. Before long, his empty chair was perpetually filled with neighbors who wanted to chat. Over time, they turned into a community through what Steve dubs "the Conversation Curve."[3]

One afternoon, my friend and I (we were the same age) were hanging out in the farmers' market parking lot. An older kid approached us with a proposition. For every ball my friend or I hit over the fence

When Keith Speaks of Hammond, Indiana, read about what Steve Bankes had done, Speaks began to promote the idea in his area. He shared the idea with the Foundations of East Chicago, which gave Neighborhoods Inc. a grant for the "Please, Have a Seat!" program. They began with thirteen benches in front yards, and they hope to have two hundred "microparks" throughout East Chicago soon.

Randy and I have done this, just trying to fill our evening hours and not return to work. In the evenings after dinner, we took two chairs, previously used at soccer and baseball games, and placed them in our front yard (we didn't have a front porch on this particular house) and sat in them with a banjo and a book. We noticed neighbors stopping by to chat. After a few nights, we brought out some extra chairs (purchased at Wal-Mart for about $7 each) and a pitcher of something to drink. We invited our neighbors to sit with us and "waste" the next hour or so. The kids played, and we conversed. We now have about fifteen of these chairs, because more and more neighbors began walking by and staying. Between the kids playing and the adults relaxing and chatting, we have had as many as twenty people in our front yard on any given evening, totally spontaneous and with no agenda. If we can be successful at this, having been unintentional about it, imagine what a little intentionality could do.

We like to use the acronym SAFE to describe what neighborhoods can and should be like: Spontaneous, Available, Fun, and Eating together. As adults, our greatest obstacle to being creative and spending time with neighbors is finding a way to carve out time and margin for it in our Hebrew Day Planner. For ideas on how to be successful, keep reading. We offer some suggestions in later chapters.

Rozanne

he would give us a dollar; for every ball he hit over the fence we would give him fifty cents. This would have been a great deal if my friend and I had been able to hit the ball over the fence, but neither of us could. Within fifteen or twenty minutes we were down fifteen dollars. It may not sound like a lot of money to the average kid today, but back in 1969 it was more than I had either on me or at home. I told this older and now scary creditor that I needed to go home and get the money — though I had no intent of coming back. I tucked myself into the innermost recesses of our duplex home and prayed. Within the hour, I heard my dad call out my name from the front porch. As happens in neighborhoods where people spend most of their time at home, there is a network that makes it hard to hide. My dad paid the young man the portion ($7.50) I owed. As my brother watched, he shook his head and laughed, communicating to me with his eyes, *If I had been with you, this never would have happened.* Of course, it never happened again.

Today, most kids only play with children their own age under a concept that might be called "arranged friendships." You've heard of arranged marriages. Well, this is similar. For a seven-year-old girl to play with another seven-year-old girl in suburbia, "arrangements" have to be made by the adults. Telephone calls are made days in advance; drop-off and pick-up details are set. Because this arrangement often involves a commute across town, the subject of spending the night is often broached. This mono-generational play system involves a high commitment to scheduling and chauffeuring on the part of parents and wipes out the value that comes from intergenerational mentoring. Shame on us!

Because children today typically play with children their own age, they only know adults the approximate age of their own parents. This, too, is extremely unfortunate — as well as potentially harmful. Some of the most significant relationships and effective mentoring opportunities come with the "in-between ages." For example, my daughter has grown up interacting, hanging out, listening to music, going on vacations, sharing meals, and participating in activities with a neighborhood family group of adults and kids of all ages. She has developed significant relationships with other girls who are three to ten years younger than she is. It is a beautiful sight. It provides wonderful leadership mentoring opportunities for my daughter. This intergenerational community has enabled my daughter to grow up with spiritual grandparents, aunts, and uncles. In turn, my wife and I have spiritual nieces and nephews of all ages.

I can usually spot a child who is being fed an unbalanced diet of age and gender friendships. Their common traits are intolerance for children of different ages and inability to hold a conversation with adults,

We've all met them. Kids who can barely look adults in the eye, let alone respond when the adult asks them a question. Sometimes they are extremely shy, but most of the time the lack of response is because the child is uncomfortable. He or she simply hasn't been around anyone older — not older children and certainly not adults who are not their parents. One of the things Randy had a vision for, particularly with our boys, was to intentionally teach our kids how to introduce themselves when they met someone new. They could do this from the time they were about seven years old. Now, at twenty-six, twenty-three, twenty-one, and eighteen, if you walk into a room where one of our boys is and he has never met you, he will come up to you, shake your hand (with a good firm grasp), and say, "Hello, I'm _____. Good to meet you." It only took one talk from Dad and a couple of simple nudges the first few times before each one started doing this on a routine basis.

Our children have also had dinner around the table with a lot of guests — their friends and ours, not to mention visitors from all over the world. They have learned to converse in a respectful manner with everyone, no matter the age. It makes it easy to take my children anywhere. As a mom, I am grateful Randy had a vision for this long before they were adults.

Rozanne

as well as high levels of discomfort in interactions with adults. They typically don't know how to share and can be downright rude. In my estimation, this is a direct outcome of an intentional parental strategy. The lifestyle many have selected for their children robs them of opportunities to experience and cultivate rich intergenerational mentoring relationships.

Lost Conflict Management Skills

As with leadership skills, activities that are driven, structured, and refereed by adults diminish opportunities for children to develop conflict management skills. If a conflict emerges on the playing field, the adults jump in quickly. Sometimes the adults handle it correctly; many times they handle it poorly, thus demonstrating that they haven't learned much about conflict management either. Many times I've seen screaming parents on the sidelines or in each other's faces at the soccer or baseball fields. This kind of negative modeling imprints destructive mechanisms for conflict resolution on children's brains to their harm later in life.

In *unstructured play*, with adults nearby but not in charge, children are put in a position to resolve conflicts, at least with regard to the hundreds of minor skirmishes that emerge each day. If a child in a circle of friends continues to abuse the group and shows no sign of changing the behavior, he or she will eventually be shunned or not invited to the circle to play anymore. However, given a chance, children will learn how to resolve most conflicts in a sandbox, in the halls at school, or on the baseball field. This will serve them well later in life. Of course, Christian parental coaching and modeling are essential components of the equation. But this is not the same as directing and controlling the resolution of the conflict.

Lost Health

Dr. Paul Rosch writes, "Childhood, as we formerly recognized it, is rapidly becoming extinct. There is less and less free time for playing with others, and learning how to develop friendships and social skills."[4]

I agree in principle, and I've also seen it with my own eyes. There is a certain sadness, and for some an almost zombielike state, in children today. The mystery and wonder of being a kid seem to be losing ground.

A whole new field of study has emerged and blossomed over the last ten years. The subject? Children and stress. An editor for *Healthy Kids* magazine writes, "Whether they're running off to child care, preschool, play dates, or after-school activities, many children today are overscheduled. While they undoubtedly benefit from a variety of activities, children can suffer from burnout and overcommitment and experience stress just like adults."[5]

The apostle Paul, author of thirteen New Testament books, writes these insightful and inspired words for modern-day parents: " 'I have the right to do anything,' you say — but not everything is beneficial" (1 Corinthians 6:12). The variety of activities we arrange for our children is not immoral and is certainly permissible for the Christian parent. But not everything we involve our kids in is beneficial for them. As a matter of fact, if carried too far, which is the case with many children today, it can have long-term negative effects on their emotional and physical health.

Your four-year-old has preschool at 9:00 a.m., a play date at 1:00 p.m., an appointment with the dentist at 3:00 p.m., and karate lessons at 4:30 p.m. Child psychologist David Elkind offers this simple observation regarding this scenario: "Sometimes children's to-do lists seem as crammed as adults'." He goes on to offer this vital caution: "Overscheduling is a major cause of stress in kids ... In the hustle and bustle, kids can miss out on two very important things — family time and solo playtime."[6]

Most parents I know — my wife and I included — have nothing but the best intentions when it comes to their children, but they are unwittingly introducing them to the same kind of stress they inflict on themselves. And, as we've seen in previous chapters, it has wreaked havoc on our lives physically and emotionally. Stress is now recognized as one of the key stimulators of cancer. This fact alone should cause us to rethink the way we approach our children's schedule. Because we are starting them earlier on this train wreck of stress, the results promise to be more devastating—a self-inflicted Armageddon, if you will.

Lost Finances

I've already suggested that it takes a lot of cash to fund this paradigm of family life. The cost of purchasing and maintaining multiple family vehicles (including the gas to run them); the cost of the fees, supplies, and equipment to play sports; the cost of buying convenience dinners; and other miscellaneous costs must all be factored into the mix. But what does this have to do with the negative impact this lifestyle has on our children? Several things come to mind, but I'll focus on what I see as the main concern.

Funding all of the activities of the children can be stressful for parents to sustain. At Christmastime, American parents often struggle to stay within a budget that matches their reasonably available income. Parents often struggle to restrain from excessive purchasing—after all, they want their children to have a great Christmas. Stress becomes a reality when the December and January credit card bills arrive.

The same stress emerges out of a difficulty to say no to the myriad of activities we're invited to enroll our kids in. Once our children's world is framed in this method, it's difficult to get out—at least partly because there seems to be no other option. If we get out, and then find we're not sufficiently convinced that the "road less traveled" is truly better, it may be hard to reenter the previous lifestyle once we stop. Our kid's spot on the team may be taken, or she may be significantly behind other children developmentally and thus find it more difficult to succeed or participate in the activity.

Most parents find it difficult to take this risk. So parents live with the stress of striving to finance the plan. Because this approach to budgeting isn't sustainable for the average single-income family, it often becomes a factor in a decision that both parents will work outside the home. When this happens, the parents often aren't available to be present at the activities—which almost guarantees the routine consumption of fast foods instead of wholesome meals that replenish the body. It also creates a chaos in scheduling, which raises the level of tension between Mom and Dad and the kids. The stress created by the financial burden is clearly felt by the children. Most of us know that minor discord between Mom and Dad is really a major stress creator for the children who observe the tension.

A simple game of organized baseball at 7:00 at night is hardly fair compensation for the number of impatient commands yelled at a child to get her to the event on time. I can't imagine the parents are having fun either. No, from experience I know they aren't! And after saying all this, I have no idea how the single parent even *begins* to play this game —yet I am utterly amazed at how many do.

Jesus gives us this word of advice to consider: "Suppose one of you wants to build a tower. Won't you first sit down and estimate the cost to see if you have enough money to complete it?" (Luke 14:28). The real cost involves not only money but also time. Failure to adequately meet the cost, coupled with an unwillingness to get out, can send the cost soaring in the form of stress and chaos that rock our kids' worlds.

Lost Family Meals

Possibly the deadliest sin of all is not what overscheduling activities does to the child but what it keeps them from. In my decade-long study of human community, I've discovered that one of the best things you can do for a child is to have consistent dinners as a family at dusk, with food that is balanced and whole and conversation that is free and slow. So convinced are we of this activity that we've devoted all of chapter 10 to it.

When I was a child, my mother always made dinner and had it on the table at the same time each day. I played summer baseball. I never remember our games or practices interfering with dinner. I don't remember a single time when my parents took us through a drive-up window for the sake of convenience. Today, children's activities have zero regard for family dinnertime.

Family dinner is not achieved simply by having food available for the family and then watching TV or sitting in different rooms to eat. Nor does it just involve everybody sitting at a table together — although this is certainly a base requirement. Conducting family dinners is a lost art. It is the centerpiece of the day, the place where family and often

My dad was an independent grocer who worked long hours Monday through Saturday — starting at 5:00 am when he left to go to the farmers' market in East Cleveland so he could ensure that the produce on his stands was the freshest he could provide for customers, and ending at 8:00 p.m. when he arrived home. And so, for the most part, he was unavailable for dinners on weeknights and Saturdays. His store was closed on Sundays, however, and we all went to church and came home to a wonderful meal my mom had prepared before she left for church or the day before. Sometimes she put a roast with potatoes and carrots in the oven; sometimes she prepared spaghetti and meatballs (our favorite).

My best memories involve times spent with my family around our table. As we became older, our table was always open for us to bring friends home and eventually our future spouses. We conversed, laughed, and lingered around good food and conversation. I had long since entered adulthood before it occurred to me how important this time was — how much we were learning as my parents interacted with each other and with us and as we kids interacted with each other. As an adult, when I go home (with our four grown children), we all look forward to Grandma's home cooking and time around the table. Many times after dinner, we wash and dry the dishes together and then come back to the table to play games and have dessert.

Many things happen at the table. It is a time when we eat healthy foods — at least healthier than fast foods or grabbing snacks from the pantry on our way out the door. The food does not have to be labor-

friends sit down and talk, catch up on the day, and tell stories. The table is the heart of community. Yet most families struggle to have one dinner together a week, and when they do, they feel awkward, not sure what to do—and therefore they are not quick to repeat the experience.

In this chapter, we've tried to demonstrate that the overcrowded

intensive to be good, and there are many wonderful options that save us time in the kitchen.

As I travel to restaurants (I love to cook but love to eat out occasionally too), one thing I've noticed is that children tend to be unruly at the table. In an article titled "Teaching Kids Table Manners," the writer worries that we are creating a generation of "table heathens."[7] As I read this article, it occurred to me that the first place a child is introduced to manners and respecting others is at the family dinner table. Skills cultivated at the table carry over into other areas of life. Is it any wonder we struggle with some of the problems with our children and teens when we have forgone the valuable evening meal where our kids are respected and learn to respect?

We have the opportunity to teach our children invaluable social skills at the table that may otherwise get overlooked. We also instill values of the importance of family (love and bonding), friends (hosting), respect (in the way we speak to and listen to each other), sharing (passing the food), working together (making sure everyone has what they need before anyone starts eating, as well as through setting up and cleaning up), and the list goes on.

We'll spend more time on this later, but don't let the busyness and fast pace of life squash one of the most important times of the day. Reclaim the mealtime and your kids! If you want a scrumptious meal to prepare for your family, see the recipe for "Mom Bitonti's Sunday Afternoon Pot Roast" at the end of the chapter. As you might suspect, it's real simple! Don't forget to take pleasure in the unfolding novel of your family's day as you enjoy the roast.

Rozanne

schedule, which develops out of good intentions, is in the end harmful to our children. Not only is it stressful; it also robs them of the experience of the connection requirement discussed in chapter 2. If we genuinely love our children and want the best for them and believe that there's validity to what's been presented in this chapter, then we need to make a change.

I'm convinced that the Hebrew Day Planner model (presented in chapter 5) provides the outline for this change. Here's what it means in a nutshell: As a general rule, all children's activities take place Monday through Saturday from 6:00 a.m. to 6:00 p.m. After this time frame, work ceases, not only for the children but also for the parents. Each evening the family enjoys dinner together, with guests invited from time to time. The cost of these meals comes from a small portion of the money saved from exiting all the previous activities. At dinner, the family and friends share the details of their day, laugh together, chew their food slowly, and tell stories. Everyone helps clean up the dinner dishes as an extension of the festival. After dinner, the conversation often continues. Some may go for a walk; a book may be read aloud or in private in the presence of others; a board game may be played; musical instruments may come out; and yes, some may watch TV for a little while. At around 10:00 p.m., the family, all present and accounted for, nestles under the covers for a peaceful night of sleep, excitedly anticipating the stories that will be told the next evening in the ongoing novel of family life.

Mom Bitonti's Sunday Afternoon Pot Roast

3 to 4 pound chuck roast
1 small bottle of (fat-free) Wishbone salad dressing
5 potatoes (can use fingerling potatoes, cut in half)
1 bunch of carrots (or you can buy a bag of baby carrots)
1 onion sliced

Marinate roast in salad dressing the night before. Place roast in a 9 x 13 glass dish sprayed with cooking spray. Cut potatoes and carrots into bite-size pieces. Place potatoes and carrots around roast and sprinkle with salt and pepper to taste. Place sliced onion on top of roast and potatoes and carrots. Put ¼ cup of water in the bottom of the dish and bake at 350 degrees for at least 3 hours. If you are home while the roast is cooking, I recommend you add the potatoes and carrots and onions in the last hour of cooking for crispier vegetables.

This recipe can be made in the Crock-Pot as well. Just cook on high for 4 hours, or on low for 7 to 8 hours.

Rozanne

|||||||||||||| DISCUSSION AND REFLECTION ||||||||||||||

1. Discuss the ways in which children's activities and schedules have changed since you were a child. Do you think things are better, worse, or about the same? What would you like to do differently?

2. This chapter presents seven ways in which our children are losing valuable character-building experience today. Pick one area that connects with you and turn it into a positive (for example, consider how you and your family could take "lost creativity" and turn it into "creative play for kids" (through pickup basketball games and the like).

      _____ lost creativity

      _____ lost leadership skills

      _____ lost mentoring

      _____ lost conflict management skills

      _____ lost health

      _____ lost finances

      _____ lost family meals

3. What did you think of the idea of creating a micropark in your community? How could you do this in your neighborhood? What elements would draw people to it? What would be your challenges?

4. Identify one personal action step you can take toward adopting a life of real simplicity.

PART 4

THE HOW-TO'S

Practical Steps to Making Room for Life

CHAPTER 9

Ten Principles of Productivity
Getting Work Done at Work

Night after night, a man came home to his family with a briefcase full of work. One evening, his little son turned to his mom as his dad once again walked in with the overstuffed briefcase in hand. "Why does Daddy always have work to do when he gets home?" he asked. His mom replied, "Because Daddy can't get it all done at the office." The boy innocently quipped back, "Why don't they put Daddy in the slower class?"

We've already established in chapter 5 that work is a very important part of our life. It is good, and it is from God. However, our work must be kept in balance with the time we take for relationships and for sleep in order for us to live healthy, happy lives. In James Patterson's best-selling novel *Suzanne's Diary for Nicholas* — the story of a busy mother and doctor named Suzanne, who is terminally ill because of a heart condition — we learn how Suzanne makes dramatic changes to structure her life in a way that balances work with relationships. As expected, she dies at a young age, and eventually her husband remarries. The stepmother finds a diary that Suzanne kept for her son, Nicholas. In the diary she finds these words of wisdom:

Imagine life is a game in which you are juggling five balls. The balls are called work, family, health, friends, and integrity. And you're keeping all of them in the air. But one day you finally come to understand that work is a rubber ball. If you drop it, it will bounce back. The other four balls—family, health, friends, and integrity—are made of glass. If you drop one of these, it will be irrevocably scuffed, nicked, or perhaps even shattered. And once you truly understand the lesson of the five balls, you will have the beginnings of balance in your life.[1]

The Hebrew Day Planner suggests that we have twelve hours of work time available to us—beginning when we get out of bed and ending when we arrive home. Therefore, 50 percent of a twenty-four-hour day is available for work and productivity—which seems like a reasonable and generous chunk of time. However, work is one of the

For those of you who (like me) do not work outside the home, don't make the mistake of skipping this chapter because you think it doesn't apply to you. As a busy stay-at-home mom with four kids, I found it easy to get my work out of balance with my relationships. Even though my most important relationships were present most of the time, so was all my work. I wanted to focus on my kids, but there was so much to be managed just to keep the house running smoothly and the kids healthy and safe. I remember many days when my kids were young that I would come to the end of a day and feel as though I had accomplished nothing. Many of the principles Randy presents in this chapter helped me keep a right perspective on my overall goals as a wife and mother and also served to make me more productive as I applied them to my work at home. After all, the hardest-working people I know are moms of small top predators of community (overscheduling our evening hours with children's activities is either number one, or it is number two to work); it preys on those precious few hours in the evening when we can be with our circle of family and friends. I'm hopeful that by now you are utterly convinced that this brand of circular social interaction is critical to your life.

Is it really possible that we can learn how to get our work done in this time frame? I want to suggest practical principles of productivity that may help this become a reality for you. Keep in mind that these principles must be learned and applied in order for them to have their full impact. Also, not every principle will be possible for everyone, given the jobs you currently have. Therefore, you may want to prioritize these in the order in which you wish to or are able to implement them, starting with the one that could have the greatest impact, given your situation.

kids. There were many evenings my husband would challenge me about my tendency to go back to work after 6:00 p.m. as I tried to get a jump start on the next day.

Through the years as I would accept projects and even work a flexible part-time job I would apply these principles. As I looked again at Making Room for Life *in anticipation of contributing to this new edition called* Real Simplicity, *this chapter has been invaluable yet again. For those of us who have a job in which we work from home, there are similar challenges to waste away the day or to let work get offside because the office is ever before us. Whether your work takes place outside your home or your office is at home, let these principles guide you as you seek to become both more balanced and productive.*

Rozanne

The Principle of Goal Setting

Setting work and career goals is a double-edged sword. In the most obvious way, it creates motivation for productivity and effectiveness. In a less obvious way, goal setting can provide boundaries and limits. When we go to work with well-defined goals, we have specific things to achieve. We are on a mission. When these things are being achieved in a reasonable time frame, we can pace ourselves in such a way so as to not burn the candle at both ends of the day—actually on either end of the day.

Effective goal setting doesn't end with establishing a goal but also includes the logical steps necessary to accomplish the goal. When we lay out more specific steps, we don't have to feel so overwhelmed with regard to the achievement of the goal.

Someone once wisely stated that "the journey of a million miles begins with but one step." I find that people who have hefty and lofty goals but who have failed to break them into bite-size daily steps often wander inefficiently through a day. This poor planning usually creates stress because work ends up having to be done in too short a time. Without question, well-defined goals can be used not only to get work accomplished but also to get you home on time.

If you work for someone, you should go over these goals ahead of time with him or her to make sure that both of you are on the same page in terms of production, quantity, and quality. Also, make sure you communicate your desire to be a serious contributor to the success of the company, but also be clear that you want to balance your work with your commitments to family and friends. Explain your desire to be home no later than 6:00 p.m. every night. Establishing well-defined goals and then measuring your accomplishment of these goals should help your supervisor work with you toward living out this worthy and balanced vision.

I work for a board of seven to nine individuals. Over the last several years, we've moved to a system of accountability through goals rather

Long-term goal setting is not my forte. At my attorney's office in my "previous life" (before kids), I was task oriented and responded to whatever my boss needed. I was always trying to make his life easier and making an effort to work ahead so he could be ready for the client or case he would be meeting with or defending. My days were spent accomplishing his goals. I had to look no further than my in-box to see what my next task was. So I carried this thinking home after I gave birth to our daughter, Jennifer. However, the demands of a little one aren't as predictable as an attorney's. There was no in-box holding my next assignment. I became the COO of our home. Day after day, I felt I was not accomplishing enough. Frustration set in as I tried to understand how I could keep an entire law office organized and running smoothly yet couldn't control my home the way I wanted to, given the demands of our precious little girl. Randy encouraged me to look at my long-term goals with Jennifer's needs in mind and determine how much I could reasonably get done in any given day and still spend the time I needed to with her. As she grew, I came to realize that there were a few things that needed to be done on a weekly basis, but most things I had been doing weekly could be done less often in order to give her the time she required.

Randy helped me focus on the big picture and not as much on the daily or weekly chores I thought I had to accomplish. While playing and reading with our daughter seemed unproductive on the daily scale, it reaped great benefits in my long-term goal of raising her. This new mind-set paid off. I began to enjoy life more. My daughter, who is now a mom, has asked me for the books she grew to love as a child and is now reading them to her daughter. They love to read together. I was able to create an overall schedule for my week without being so structured that there was no margin to handle a sick baby who needed to go to the doctor or who required some extra attention.

Rozanne

than hours on the clock. At the beginning of the year I present a list of goals I will seek to accomplish. Once these are approved, I can go to work. I now have the freedom to manage my work in such a way that I provide excellent service as well as pace myself to ensure that there is room for a healthy dose of community and conversation. For example, we've established that I will preach on thirty-five of the fifty-two Sundays in a calendar year. On each of these weeks, preparing a quality sermon is a top priority.

The Principle of the To-Do List

Having well-defined goals that meet with your supervisor's approval, accompanied by the intent to achieve the goals with excellence and in a timely manner, opens the door to getting home at or before 6:00 p.m. However, we must go one step further. We must create a daily to-do list from these stated goals a day or even a week in advance.

One member of my congregation has lived the Hebrew Day Planner concept religiously for years. One of the things he has done masterfully is to write down on a simple 3 x 5 card the top three things he must get done during the work hours of daylight. When he is done with these three items, his workday is over. Because these things are carefully chosen the day before and because he is disciplined, he hardly ever struggles to be done by 6:00 p.m. As a matter of fact, he's usually done before noon. I've known this man for twenty years, and I believe he may be the most successful, de-stressed person I know.

Be careful not to dismiss this principle just because you don't think you have this kind of freedom. We can all learn from this productivity principle, no matter what our job. I mentioned above that I have a shared goal with my church's elder council that I will speak a minimum of thirty-five Sunday mornings a year. Because this is my number one job responsibility, it is the first item on my to-do list for Monday morning. I stay home so that I'll avoid highly stimulating conversations with my staff members. Eight out of ten times, the sermon is done by the end of the workday on Monday (6:00 p.m.). On at least five of these eight occasions, the sermon is completed by 2:00 p.m. I spent the first eight years of pastoral ministry on a schedule that would get me home well after 6:00 p.m. and would leave me stressed-out at the end of the week — often, in fact, without a sermon! The irony was that on Sunday morning I was going to stand up and tell my congregation how to live the Christian life, and yet on Monday through Saturday night my attitude suggested that I knew very little about the subject.

Writing out a to-do list is an age-old practice that many of my friends and acquaintances don't do very well. However, my goal is not that you become proficient at establishing a highly honed to-do list the day before so that you can get more work done in a given day; rather, I desire for you to be a responsible steward for God, your employer, and

I am queen of the to-do list. Actually, I would create a list that is as long as the year is and keep it going. I love to check off jobs, feeling a sense of success as I go. As a matter of fact, I would add things to my list like "brush my teeth" just so I could check it off. Seriously, I have had to learn to apply this principle to my work in my home, as well as to ministry and writing opportunities accepted. Now, instead of writing a to-do list of everything I can think of that I need to do, I simply write down the top two or three things that need to be done that day, and when they are finished, so am I. While I may have a longer list on my computer, the ones I write out on a 3 x 5 card are the only ones I keep right in front of me. Usually there is a goal for ministry, for a domestic project that will move our family ahead, for a domestic chore (something that needs to be routinely done), and for a project or work-related activity. Doing this keeps me from becoming overwhelmed by the larger goal and allows me to retain focus. Having used this principle many times for ministry projects, it has served to keep me balanced and sane.

Rozanne

your family by being productive during the work hours so you can be faithful to enter into the relationship season (6:00 p.m. – 10:00 p.m.) successfully without feeling guilty.

The Four-Hour Principle

Specialists tell us that the most gifted of us only get a total of four hours of effective work done in any given day. While we may spend eight, ten, or twelve hours at the office, when all the chaff is separated from the pure wheat, there are only four hours worth of highly productive labor on the table. (I think that four hours may be a bit too generous.)

How does this principle help us live out the Hebrew Day Planner more consistently? If embraced, it dispels the notion that spending more time in the office is the solution to our productivity problems. Many people believe they're showing that they take their work seriously if they

I guess you could say I'm a type B personality. Most people want to be a type A, but that just has never been in the cards for me. Randy can run his life at seventy miles per hour (or at least he could; he has now slowed to about fifty miles per hour), but I am good at a steady forty miles per hour. Because I run at a slower pace, it is important that I choose to do this segment of work during a part of the day when I'm fresh and unhindered by the stress of preparing a meal or rushing out to pick up the kids. If I am feeling tired, I'm unproductive, not to mention grumpy.

During those years when my children were little, I would consistently run out of steam about the dinner hour. I couldn't wait to go to sleep right after I put the kids down for bed at about 7:30. This wasn't good for my marriage. I was just plain tired all the time and prone to becoming irritated. Randy would encourage me to take a nap during the day, but I thought I needed to use the kids' nap time as a time to get more things done.

stay longer at the workplace. This is simply not true. Rather, we should seek to consolidate our four hours of effective work within the tightest framework we can — six to eight hours certainly seems achievable.

The Principle of Giftedness

One of two principles seems to be at work: (1) Because there are areas of my job where I am not gifted, time flows toward my weaknesses and I seldom get to do what I am truly gifted at doing. (2) My time flows toward what I am gifted in and passionate about, but because my job includes more than this, I am constantly falling behind and getting stressed-out. Either one of these scenarios can leave a person feeling overworked and overwhelmed. In order to balance your work with your relationships and your sleep time, you must find a remedy.

The ideal solution is to define as much of your job as you can in

One day, however, I ran into a good friend at the grocery store who asked me if I was tired. I admitted I was. Knowing the stage of life I was in, she said, "Rozanne, you have to get your rest. You do know that during World War II, the Chinese and the KGB used sleep deprivation as torture, don't you?" Armed with a new perspective, I finally had the courage to accept Randy's encouragement. I began to take naps at least a few days a week so I had the alertness to squeeze a bit more productivity into my day and still have a little time with Randy in the evenings. Now that my children are grown, although regular naps are not necessary, I still find it wonderful to lie down on a Sunday afternoon and relax. Sometimes I sleep; sometimes I just rest. But I always find that it changes my attitude and productivity for the entire week. Life runs in seasons. If you have little kids, let me give you permission to take a nap when your kids do, so that you can be at your best for your family and for your relational time. They'll be glad you did!

Rozanne

your realm of giftedness. The thought is simple: You are most valuable and productive when you work in your area of giftedness. The second justification is that you are most fulfilled and efficient when you work within the scope of your giftedness.

Here is the challenge: How do you identify the center of your giftedness and find a job that needs what you do best and pays you a decent wage to do it? If you are able to put this principle into practice in your life, you should enter corporate worship each Sunday with a grateful heart, eager to express your worship and bring your financial gifts to God, because very few people are able to make this principle work.

However, you must be careful to place boundaries on the amount of work you do under this arrangement. The more passionate you are

I have found this principle to be true in every ministry and job I have taken on. When I have undertaken a task not within the scope of my giftedness, it drains me significantly, not only making me tired but discouraged and frustrated as well. When I accept an assignment within my giftedness, I am always energized by it (perhaps feeling tired but excited and refreshed at the same time).

I remember the day I was asked to serve on our school's PTA. I was honored (flattered really; there is a difference) they would ask me since my daughter was only a kindergartner. The woman said she thought I would be a good asset to the team. What an ego booster! I spent the next year of my life dreading the meetings and overwhelmed by the assignments while trying to balance my responsibilities with my husband and three little kids. It drained me.

On the other hand, I have served in a ministry for deaf persons for years. While it is a more time-consuming position, I am excited and come home energized every time I've been with my deaf friends. The difference is that God created me with a love for languages and for people. I have the opportunity to express who I am in Christ when I serve.

about your work and the more praise you receive from others, the greater the temptation to extend the time you spend doing it. Our human nature causes us to move toward that which we feel competent doing. If you currently feel awkward and unsuccessful around your family and friends, you may subconsciously avoid the extensive encounters recommended by the Hebrew Day Planner. This should not encourage us to move away from the principle of giftedness, but we should seek to use it wisely to encourage balance in our lives.

Applying the first four principles of productivity reads like this: (1) We should seek to work the greatest portion of our day within our area of giftedness; (2) we should mutually agree on our goals with our supervisor or board; (3) the day before we come to work, we should

Although I believe (and know from experience) that God may call someone to do a task that does not fit exactly with their skill set (far be it from me to limit God), I find most of the time if I am in a situation that doesn't fit with my strengths, it is usually because I mistook the ego strokes for a nudge from the Holy Spirit. I needed to learn how to say no. Or at least, "Let me pray about this before I give you an answer." Now if someone asks me to do something, I respond appropriately. If I can't say, "No, this isn't what I'm cut out for," or "No, this particular project takes skills that are not in my set," then I ask for time to pray about it and talk to Randy before I make the commitment. More than once, we decided together that God wasn't calling me to a given assignment. Randy does the same with me if he is considering a huge undertaking. This type of communication brings confirmation to the commitment and enables our spouse and partner to have ownership and be more willing to support through an assignment's tough times. If you are single — and especially a single parent — I encourage you to find a close friend or relative who can help you in putting this principle into practice.

Rozanne

develop the top three or four things we need to do to achieve our goals; and (4) what we plan to accomplish should be reasonably achieved in four hours, leaving additional time for unavoidable distractions, breaks, and administrative requirements.

The Principle of Delegation and Teamwork

This principle of productivity, if effectively applied, can help us get all the necessary work done within a healthy allotment of time (6:00 a.m. to 6:00 p.m.). If teamwork could be formed on the basis of a balance of gifts and if everyone knew and respected each other's gifts and unique contributions, more work could be done in less time.

Three things have to happen for this principle to be activated. First, we must know our own gifts and competencies. Second, we must know the gifts and competencies of each member of our team. Third, we must organize and delegate the work according to this giftedness and commitment to teamwork. It would be wise for every team to discover

This is a valuable principle when applied to the work in the family. Each member in a family has a contribution to make to the overall well-being of the whole. It is also a gift to our children to enable them to realize that they are part of a team and that their skill set is needed and valued. Often our kids have talents and skills we parents don't. This is the beauty of how God creates each individual uniquely. I wish I had realized some of my daughter's skills earlier. (Sorry, Jenn, I learned how to parent on you.) She is highly creative and gifted when it comes to decorating, gift giving, and creating a beautiful environment. I am not! I just called her because I had an inspiration for our Christmas tree but had no idea how to pull it off. She went to the store and bought the supplies — and the whole project was finished in fifteen minutes.

Rozanne

and apply these necessary steps. When applied, this plan yields intense productivity.

It has been my experience that every effective team needs three kinds of workers: influencers, contributors, and managers. Influencers create and cast vision. Contributors do the frontline work. Managers train, equip, and support the team of contributors to get the work done. When a team has people placed according to their design, productivity skyrockets. When people are placed out of whack with their giftedness, no number of hours invested will allow a team to experience long-term economic or missional viability.

The Principle of Positional Identity

The classic movie *Chariots of Fire* tells the story of two men who competed in the 1924 summer Olympics and won gold medals (Harold Abrahams in the 100-meter race and Eric Liddell in the 400-meter race). However, they ran for different reasons. Abrahams ran to prove to himself and to the world that he was someone who should be taken seriously. This is understandable, given the difficulty that Jewish people had in being accepted in Christian cultures in those days. But what a stressful way to live! Eric Liddell, on the other hand, ran to express who he was. He is quoted as saying, "When I run, I feel God's pleasure."

Liddell is expressing one of the most powerful benefits of the Christian life—the principle of *positional identity*. This axiom of faith is built on the foundation that, when a person believes in and receives Jesus Christ as Savior, he or she becomes a child of God (John 1:12). This new identity is not granted because of our performance but because of the perfect performance of Jesus on our behalf (John 3:16; Ephesians 2:8–9). If the Christian disciple comes to understand and embrace this principle as a way of life, it will dramatically affect his or her work life. Each morning as we wake up to face the day, the issue of *who we are* is not up for grabs. Our mission becomes to *express* who we are, not to *prove* to others who we are.

How does this principle work to make us more productive? When a person is secure in who he or she is and positively seeks to express it through work, there is a greater likelihood of avoiding addiction to work, praise, or competition, as well as the unhealthy climbing of the corporate ladder in areas outside of our giftedness. For those who look to their work for a sense of identity (instead of expressing their identity through their work), their lives can become as pitiful as that of dogs begging for table scraps. It is a shameless pursuit. Many people in this position—or lack of position—struggle to keep their work lives in balance with cultivating relationships and getting the necessary sleep.

The Principle of Commute Reduction

The Hebrew Day Planner architecture calls for production to be done from 6:00 a.m. to 6:00 p.m. Included in this block of time is the commute to and from work. With many people experiencing one-hour commutes each way, it makes it difficult to get to work, do the work expected of you, and return home—all by 6:00 p.m.

There are, I believe, five possible solutions.

Move closer to work. Over the last fourteen years, my family has made a commitment to consider our places of work in our selection of a home. We've lived in two places in the same town during these years, and both of these places have been less than five miles from my office. This has not only reduced the stress of traffic jams and road rage but has also added to my available time for work one to three hours a day, or up to fifteen hours a week.

Go to and leave work when the traffic is light. In north central Texas, if you want to head into Dallas from Arlington, you have to leave either before 6:30 a.m. or after 8:45 a.m. The same principle applies on the way home: leave either at or before 4:00 p.m. or wait until after 6:30 p.m. Of course, I'm in favor of leaving early and coming home early in order to meet the requirement of the Hebrew Day Planner. Talk to your supervisor and see if you can work out a suitable arrangement. Many companies utilize flextime, which makes it easy for the employee to adjust to the Hebrew Day Planner.

Use public transportation. Many suburbs have a train, subway, or busing system that allows you to ride on a strict schedule and get work done while traveling to and from your office. The key is to follow a schedule, reserving for the commute the kind of work you can do on a train.

Work at home. This may not sound like an attractive option, but you may want to consider it as the lesser of two evils—scrambling like crazy to try to be home at 6:00 p.m. and avoiding stress-filled traffic jams, or finding a quiet and motivating spot to work at home. More companies are providing this option as a way to reduce the overhead cost of office space. Certain cities in California, such as in the Silicon Valley area, offer tax incentives to companies that can keep their employees off the congested roadway systems. Look for planned communities in the near future that promote this feature of working at home or in an office complex within walking distance of many homes.

If you can't work at home every day, see if you can do it two or three days a week. Don't be surprised to discover the same thing homeschoolers have discovered: *It doesn't take all day to get your work done.* Many reasonably disciplined children who are homeschooled get their work done by noon or 1:00 p.m. each day. Studies show that a great number of them are outstripping their conventional schoolmates in academic achievements and are being admitted into North America's top colleges and universities.

Change jobs. This may sound crazy—and it may not be possible—but don't dismiss it too quickly. If you embrace the shift from a lifestyle of accumulation to a lifestyle of conversation—and if you originally chose your job because of the compensation that allowed you to finance a chosen consumer lifestyle—then it makes sense to reconsider your decision if the premise changed. At the very least, if commuting long distances each day is an issue for you and you can't apply the first four ideas, this is something that deserves serious consideration. Insanity is doing the same thing over and over again, expecting all the while vastly different results. Do something different for a change.

The Principle of Results for Flexibility

This principle has already been expressed above in the example of seeking permission to reduce your commute time by changing the times you go to and leave the office in order to avoid traffic congestion. However, this principle is significant enough to deserve its own space.

Our assistant works full-time. She is married and has two teenage daughters. We want to see her live a balanced life, and thus we're open to the "results for flexibility" principle. She promises to deliver defined results while we offer flexibility. She drops her daughters off at school at 7:30 a.m. and gets to the office at 7:45. On Tuesday, Wednesday, and Thursday, her goal is to leave at 5:30 p.m. If she accomplishes what she needs to get done, she sometimes leaves earlier, which we support. On Monday and Friday, she leaves at 2:30 p.m. to pick up her daughters from school. If she still has a few things to get done, she'll plan her day so they can be done at home. However, our goal is that she'll have everything done at 2:30.

When you have a person with her outstanding work ethic and ability to manage priorities, a boss would be foolish to forbid this structure. At the end of the day, she feels in charge of her life and refreshed, grateful to have the opportunity to enjoy the work God has given her to do while balancing work with relationships and the need for sleep. Results-oriented people are the kind of people whom bosses should seek to hire; every employee should seek to be a results-oriented person.

The Principle of Outsourcing

Rozanne and I have four children. As she and I looked at our schedule from week to week, we began to notice that there were two time-consuming things on the agenda that we wanted to eliminate. Don't be shocked at their uniqueness: doing the yard work and cleaning the house. What if we could outsource these tasks? Impossible! After all, that's only available to the superrich. While this suggestion is out of the reach for some at certain seasons of life (like college students — who probably don't own houses with lawns — or newlyweds), it deserves consideration if we want to make the shift from accumulation to conversation and still live in suburbia.

Here's what we came up with as a solution. The average monthly car payment in our area is around $400 a month. For a large family like ours, the cost of a seven- or eight-passenger vehicle can easily be $700 or $800 a month. What if we diligently saved enough money to pay cash for a reliable used car (reliable to us means that it can have high miles as long as it's been well serviced and has records to prove it) and then used the freed-up cash to purchase time? While it may differ from community to community, we've been able to find excellent services to clean our house once a week and to care for our lawn once a week for around $400 a month. Because our commuting is drastically less than the average family, the used, paid-off cars we drive, if routinely serviced, do a fine job of getting us from point A to point B.

Why do outsourcing services such as housecleaning and yard work sound lavish and pretentious, but owning a brand-new automobile that depreciates in value daily seems like a nonnegotiable purchase and the inalienable right of all Americans? I suggest that the journey of moving from accumulation to conversation sees things differently.

The Principle of Efficiency

This final principle, while self-evident, can do as much as any of the other principles to make us more productive in less time, so that we can experience daily the kind of relational community we were designed to experience.

The principle of efficiency essentially seeks to perpetually answer this question about everything we do at work: *How can this be done in less time?* This may not apply to the aging of wine, but it applies to most things I can think of that must be done in the workplace. Simply make a list of the things you do and seek to find a more efficient way to do it. I recommend that you seek counsel from others.

I once heard the true story of a man who decided to go to his annual homeowners' association meeting. They were having problems with beavers eating the trees. A motion was made by the chairperson to replace the trees eaten by the beavers. How crazy! The only reason you'd want to do this is if you had a mission to feed the lifestyle of beavers. But if your desire is to efficiently solve this problem, the correct solution is to refrain from planting trees until you take care of the beavers.

My wife and I purchased our first washer and dryer in 1983 when we bought our first home. With routine maintenance, these appliances were still running twenty years later. With a family of six, washing clothes is a major chore and a significant investment of time. My wife's biggest problem was having to run the dryer for two or three complete cycles in order for the clothes to dry, which involved a lot of waiting and a lot of stress. Because we don't do work in our home after 6:00 p.m. — including washing clothes — we decided we needed to look for a solution to this problem.

We zeroed in on the pursuit of efficiency as a possible answer. We discovered that it was possible to buy a new washer and dryer for about the same price we paid for our current set. However, it would result in just a slight improvement. We then found a set that cost twice the money but supposedly used less water during the washing cycle so that the clothes weren't as wet when put into the new, more powerful, efficient dryer. The sales pitch was that the dryer would be done drying before the next load of clothes was done washing. That was just what we were looking for!

So in the course of considering the purchase, we checked with a few people who owned this model to see if the salesperson was giving us the true story. To our amazement he was. I took a calculator and determined that our current set was costing us about $40 a year. Using the same formula we concluded that the new set would cost us $80 a year, or $1.54 cents a week. Here was the deciding question: *Would we be willing to spend $1.54 a week for my wife and the mother of four children to gain back twelve hours of time a week?* This is an astounding value of thirteen cents an hour. The decision was made. I just confirmed with my wife a few minutes ago that the plan is still working.

The motive for presenting these ten principles of productivity is not to increase work volume but rather to accomplish the work that needs to be done—and to do it within the totally reasonable twelve hours of allotted time—so that you can experience the wonderful conversation

---

One of the best ways I've found to aid efficiency is to plan my meals for the week. If I can sit down and go through my coupons, recipes, and grocery ads for about thirty minutes a week, I save not only time but money as well. I make one trip to the grocery store instead of five or six. I like to post my menu where the whole family (and at times those who live with us temporarily) can see it and make their plans accordingly and let me know if they aren't going to be there on a given evening. This has worked beautifully. My kids know when I'll be preparing a meal they would like to invite their friends for—or if they are planning a date, they can miss a meal they don't particularly like! A great aid in preparing the right amount of food, which also saves money.

The second most efficient thing I've learned to do is to group my errands. The further you live from your stores, the more necessary this becomes. I already mentioned that when we lived in Chicago, I could do all my errands within the scope of about a one-mile radius. However, we now live between San Antonio and a little town called Boerne. I need to run all my errands in Boerne at the same time. When I have a hair appointment or a doctor appointment in San Antonio, I make sure I head to my favorite mall over there. Efficiency planning makes and keeps my life much simpler!

Rozanne

---

and community with family and friends that God intended for you. Work is an important ball to juggle, but we must remember that it is only a rubber ball, while family, health, friends, and integrity are balls made of glass. Or, to put it another way, the goal is not to make a living but to make room for living.

|||||||||||||||||| DISCUSSION AND REFLECTION ||||||||||||||||||

1. Which of the ten principles of productivity are difficult for you? Which ones are you most gifted at executing?

_____ the principle of goal setting

_____ the principle of the to-do list

_____ the four-hour principle

_____ the principle of giftedness

_____ the principle of delegation and teamwork

_____ the principle of positional identity

_____ the principle of commute reduction

_____ the principle of results for flexibility

_____ the principle of outsourcing

_____ the principle of efficiency

2. How does positional identity (your security in who you are and who God made you to be) play into how you plan your days and even your priorities? How does it affect your to-do list, the jobs and ministries you take on, and so forth? Be honest.

3. Identify one personal action step you can take toward adopting a life of real simplicity.

Discovering the Convivium
The Importance of Sharing a Meal

What if every member of the family completed their work on Monday through Saturday between the hours of 6:00 a.m. and 6:00 p.m.? What if a family, and even a collection of people living in the same neighborhood, tried to live by the principle that all work ceased after 6:00 p.m.? No housework, laundry, e-mails, reports, home projects, homework, organized sports — and no evening meetings at church.

This has become the lifestyle of my family and a growing number of families that want to exit the chaotic lifestyles, reclaim our lives, and connect with the circle of people God has given us. The Hebrew Day Planner (see chapter 5) provides a broad guide to accomplish this lifestyle. As in an exercise program, we falter and flex, but we always come back to the plan in the belief that it will replenish our souls.

From the time our family made this commitment to the time it became the new rhythm for our life together was a period of roughly two years. As mentioned in chapter 6, old habits die hard. Everything seems to favor the status quo, even if we know it is harming us. There were, and still are, many causes, activities, and temptations that seek to pull us back into the lifestyle that promises so much but in the end gives so little.

For our family, housework has been the easiest area to address. My wife, who has a disciplined personality, works a part-time job outside the home that has a flexible schedule. She has formulated a schedule so she can shop, do laundry, and run errands during the 6:00 a.m. to 6:00 p.m., Monday through Saturday, time frame.

My work is another area that has finally come together. One of the driving forces for this adjustment is the fear of repeating the forty-five days of sleepless nights I experienced several years ago. Fear is sometimes a healthy motivator. Knowing that work will cease at 6:00 p.m. causes me to be more intentional and efficient with regard to how I use my day.

The third area to come under alignment was church. Gratefully, we had begun years ago to transition our church from a central campus program model to a place-based community model (see my previous book *The Connecting Church*). Deconstructing the dozens of linear circles and offering what was worthwhile to the decentralized place-based communities was a daunting task, but today we, individually and corporately, are reaping the benefits. Spiritual work is happening throughout the week; it is just happening within the neighborhood rather than at the church facility. Last night a neighbor stopped by, with a ten-minute notice, to discuss plans for celebrating the Passover meal as a community. We discussed the action items casually in my living room for about thirty minutes and then spent another thirty minutes pondering ways God may be calling this precious lady to use her gifts and passions in the future. Some may call this a meeting, but it feels very different to me.

Without question, the most difficult area to align has been our children's activities. Children's activities are simply not family friendly. For the first time in our family's history, we have said no to spring baseball leagues. It was amazing the well-intentioned pressure we received from coaches and other parents, but we stood by our guns. The Frazee family will not be sitting outside on a school night until 10:00 p.m. watching our children play a game, knowing that they haven't finished their homework. Funny thing, our boys haven't said one word about it.

(Chapter 12 will present practical ideas on how to deal with issues like children's sports and work.)

One of the reasons some people resist this model is that they're not sure what they'll do with the time together once it is successfully freed up. You may recall from chapter 7 that this was one of the biggest concerns for the town of Ridgewood, New Jersey, as they collectively took a night off from all activity. What would they do with each other? There are some families that don't spend thirty minutes together on a regular basis, so how could they envision four hours! This chapter lays out the new vision—simple but profound in the results.

The relational season of the day (the beginning of the day for the Hebrew) lasts from 6:00 p.m. to 10:00 p.m. It is divided into two parts: 6:00 p.m. to 8:00 p.m. (the time for the meal) and 8:00 p.m. to 10:00 p.m. (open time).

The Meal

The table is the centerpiece and heart of community. This is an ancient belief—a tradition that has stood the test of time. The "real simplicity" vision is an invitation to come to the table, to share a meal and conversation with a circle of family and friends each evening. When we wake up each day to face the wonderful work that is before us, whether it takes place at school, the office, the factory, the farm, or the home, we do so with a longing—a genuine passion to gather at the table at dusk to partake of a meal that sustains us and to listen to another page in the novel of the people God has graciously brought into our lives. When this event takes place, our souls send a signal to our minds that this is right. Something in us tells us that this is a major demonstration of the connection requirement we were designed to reach. It is no mistake that Jesus chose the meal as the place where the community remembers his saving work on the cross.

Some call it "the convivium." *Convivium* is the Latin word for "feast." The convivium invites us to feast on whole foods that nourish our body and to feast on the conversation of those who sit around the sacred table of community, and thus to nourish our minds and souls. The proponents of the convivium are sometimes known as supporters of the "slow-food movement" for two reasons. First, the food is good for us and worth savoring. Second, and more important, this is the moment we've been looking forward to all day. It is the prize, the reward, for a day of hard work. When one's definition of success is measured in accumulation, then the meal has little value other than to be the fuel to keep us working until we have all the stuff we think we need or until our debts are paid off. Comedian George Carlin stated that under this arrangement "a house is just a pile of stuff with a cover on it."[1] However, when one's definition of success is conversation, then the meal becomes the end, not merely the means. Discovering the convivium is at the core of our trading of accumulation and activity for conversation and community as a way of life. With this vision, the house becomes a place of safety, replenishment, and refuge with a cover on it. In simple terms, to miss the meal, or to rush it, can only spell failure.

This is not the experience of most people I know. We are the "Fast Food Nation." The fast-food movement emerged out of the development of the superhighway system and the suburb. In 1956, Congress passed the Interstate Highway Act under the leadership of President Dwight D. Eisenhower. He had pushed hard for such a bill because he had been enormously impressed by Adolf Hitler's Reichsautobahn, the world's first superhighway system.[2] This new roadway system gave birth to the fast-food industry. Along these highways, fast-food restaurants popped up to serve a "liberated" people on the move. How has this changed the way we eat and live? Eric Schlosser, author of the bestselling book *Fast Food Nation: The Dark Side of the All-American Meal*, provides this alarming report:

- In 1970, Americans spent about $6 billion on fast food; in 2001, they spent more than $110 billion.

- Americans now spend more money on fast food than on higher

education, personal computers, computer software, or new cars.
They spend more on fast food than on movies, books, magazines,
newspapers, videos, and recorded music combined.

- On any given day in the United States about one-quarter of the
adult population visits a fast-food restaurant.

- An estimated one in three workers in the United States has at
some point been employed by McDonald's.

- What we eat has changed more in the last forty years than in the
previous forty thousand.

- The Golden Arches are now more widely recognized than the
Christian cross.[3]

While some fast food is rather tasty, it is rarely good for you, and
it is rarely eaten at home around the dinner table. Very few people can
envision pulling out the family dishes and sitting around the dining
room table with a Big Mac or a Big Beef Burrito! Fast food is made fast
and eaten fast, usually in the car on the way to an activity.

If we desire a life of real simplicity, we must discover the convivium.
We must return to a time when food is placed back on the table — and
it is worth eating slowly — and where conversation is not rushed. There
is a movement begun in Italy called "the convivium" — a growing group
of people around the world who are proactive in promoting the return
of the slow-food movement. There are currently sixty-three chapters of
the convivium in the United States.

Food Preparation

I have the wonderful blessing of being married to an Italian woman
who has worked hard to perfect her culinary skills. She was taught the
basic elements of cooking from her family and has built on it to provide
our family with a wide array of healthy food. Coming to the table at the
Frazee household is always a treat. One of the things we've lost with the

onset of the fast-food movement is the training of the next generation of cooks. (By the way, the art of cooking doesn't have to be limited to women. In several families I know, men are the primary chefs, and they do it quite well.)

One of the keys to a good meal is that it must be wholesome and good for the body. The meal doesn't have to be elaborate or fancy — although this is certainly encouraged. If no one in your family knows how to cook a full meal, I encourage you to see who can take on this important role. It can certainly be shared. If you have children, it's important to pass down this art so that their families will have access to the convivium in the future. If there is not a full meal placed on the table, it is less likely that people will gather around it for very long. In *The Rituals of Dinner,* Margaret Visser tells us that "the average length of an American dinner, with or without TV, is thirty minutes, which suggests that not a great deal of discussion is taking place."[4]

Consider alternatives as you learn to cook or have limited time to cook. One option is to find a handful of simple recipes that are wholesome and good for you, and cook in large quantities and freeze the meals. There are several cookbooks that show you how to do all of your cooking in one day a month (see, for example, *Frozen Assets*). Entire cookbooks are devoted to Crock-Pot recipes that enable you to start a meal in the morning (see, for example, *The Slow Cooker Ready and Waiting Cookbook*). Cooking Light publishes the *5 Ingredient 15 Minute Cookbook*, which includes ninety-four delicious quick-to-fix dinners for the family.[5] (FYI: my wife has stood over my shoulder for this entire paragraph.)

One of the best options, whether you are a gourmet cook or a beginner, may be to share a meal with neighbors. The workload is spread out and the conversation is expanded. You should do this at least once a week, if not twice a week. It's also great for people who are single, for single parents, and for empty nesters. With only two people in the house there is a tendency to skip a quality meal or go out to eat regularly. I believe taking the time to sit down to a meal with conversation is a better option. Whatever your approach or situation, preparing a meal for the convivium takes planning and intentionality. If you wait until the last minute, your dinner experience will almost invariably be pushed to fast food instead of slow food.

Setting the Table

After 6:00 p.m. all work should cease. Therefore, if the table is not set by 6:00, this act is not one person's responsibility but a part of the overall festival of the meal—a family affair, in other words. If you live in a home with a kitchen table and a dining room table, I strongly recommend you have your dinners in the dining room. We purposely bought a table for the kitchen that only accommodates four chairs comfortably, which forces us, as a family of six, to hold dinners in our dining room. I am convinced this will be one of the strongest memories my children have after they leave the home. (Eating outside whenever possible is ideal too. I love eating a great meal outside.)

What is set on the table should become a unique mark of each family. If your personality leans toward that of a Martha Stewart, then go all out. No matter what your bent is, though, you should seek to be creative and build traditions. For our family, we enjoy picking out unique dishes—with no particular need for everything to perfectly match. As we travel we like to pick up unique things for use at the dinner table. Each piece, whether it holds bread or pepper or vegetables, has a special place in our hearts and brings back memories each time it is used. After ten years or so, what is on your dinner table will remind your family that you have a history together—even before a single word is spoken.

On Saying Grace

I grew up in an unchurched home. When I became a Christian in 1974 at the age of fourteen, I had to make arrangements to get to church and back home by myself. The church was about a twenty-minute drive from my house. If I wanted to come back for Sunday evening worship, which I always did, it made the most sense to stay at church all afternoon or to go home with a family that lived near the church. There was one particularly gracious Italian family that invited me to their house almost every Sunday for a great meal—usually pasta and salad. The father was a successful independent grocer who had many tales of buying and selling produce that captured my attention.

At dinnertime we would gather around the table and he would "say grace." This was a new experience for me. This successful man would bow his head and humbly thank God for providing the food we were about to eat. I had never heard of such a thing. It seemed to me that he had worked very hard to get to where he was and that he should take all the credit. However, he humbled himself in the presence of his family and declared his gratitude to God. There were times when everyone else's head was bowed and eyes were closed, and I'd look up and stare at him. I desperately wanted to grow up and be like him. I wanted to raise a family and demonstrate God's love and protection on our family, just as this father did.

Well, I've been married to his beautiful daughter now for almost thirty years, and I see it as a great honor each night to say grace on behalf of my family of six. I concur with the heart of William Shakespeare, who wrote, "O Lord, that lends me life, lend me a heart replete with thankfulness."[6] Alda Ellis, in her heartwarming book *A Table of Grace*, writes this:

> The family dinner is indeed a legacy to be passed on from one generation to the next. I believe that it is more important for our children to know who the head of the family is than who the head of the country is. So many positive things begin while seated at the dinner table—respect, good communication skills, proper table manners, the humble thanking of God for our blessings.[7]

On most nights we simply hold hands, and I offer the grace. On certain nights we will ask a member of the family to do the honors. If we have guests at the table, we always pray for God's blessings on them. If a member of our family is missing from the table, we always pray for their safe return to us. On many nights we observe Communion. We have matzo crackers in the buffet next to the dinner table. At the beginning of the meal I pass around the cracker, and everyone breaks off a piece. A member of the family then says grace but focuses the prayer on the sacrifice of Jesus on the cross—the ultimate act of grace on our behalf. At the end of the meal and conversation, I pass around a goblet of wine that sits by my place setting, and every person sitting at the table takes a drink—and so we close the meal focused on the blood of Christ. Saying grace is an essential part of the Christian convivium.

The Art of Dinner Table Conversation

The dramatist W. S. Gilbert once said, "It isn't so much what's on the table that matters as what is on the chairs."[8] Jacques Pépin, chef for Oprah Winfrey, makes this observation about the importance of family meals:

> My daughter is twenty-six years old, and when she comes home, we eat together as we always have. I know people who probably haven't had a conversation with their children for years, because the children come home, say, "Hi, Dad," and go straight to the refrigerator for a sandwich. The dinner table should be the stage where you talk at the end of the day. The conversation may not always be pleasant—maybe you have an argument about what happened in school—but it is a very necessary thing that brings the family together.
>
> Food, and the sharing of food, sustains human relationships more than anything else, including sex. It's an extraordinarily important part of the family structure and the common denominator that brings people together in a house—certainly in mine! Maybe it sounds corny, but for me, food is an expression of love,

because you always cook for "the other" — wife, child, lovers, friends. Food is life.[9]

Conversations around the dinner table are not a new idea. In *The Rituals of Dinner,* Margaret Visser gives a history lesson:

> Plato's great dialogue, *Symposium*, Xenophon's *Symposium*, Plutarch's *Symposiacs* and *Banquet of the Seven Sages*, Macrobius's *Saturnalia* were the ancestors of collections of *Table Talk* or *Propos de table* which have continued as a minor tradition of European *belles lettres* down the centuries. Athenaeus wrote what must be one of the longest versions on record: fifteen volumes of chat, called *The Sophists at Dinner.*[10]

Dinner-table conversation is a lost art and practice in our society. Yet it is the thing we should long for with great intensity. While there is much written on how we should approach this conversation ("Rules and Orders of the Coffee House of 1674," for example),[11] we need not make it so complicated that today's novice is overwhelmed and avoids it altogether. At its most profound and simplest level, conversation at the dinner table involves each person sharing what happened during that day. I believe a significant part of the connection requirement is met when we have a chance to share the events of our day, no matter how mundane, with a circle of family and friends who are hanging on each word we say because they genuinely care about our welfare and are interested in our story.

Here is how it works in our family. After we've said grace and the food is on each person's plate, we simply tell about our day. We start with the family member or friend sitting on my left. Each person starts with the time they got up and then chronologically unfolds the details. When we first made the decision to do this, I wasn't sure my children would cooperate. Would my teenage daughter share her day with her younger brothers, or would she be willing to listen to them share their day the way boys share? Would they really be interested in the details of

Mom's and Dad's day in such a way that this was a meaningful experience for us? Would everyone get tired of it and do it only to placate my desire to have a dinner that lasted more than fifteen to thirty minutes?

I've been amazed at the value of this simple experience. I remember coming home one day and asking one of our sons to tell me how his day went. He responded back, "Oh, I'm saving it for dinner tonight!" We had once had an evening when we didn't tell about our day, and one of our sons asked the next afternoon if he could share stories of two days at dinner since we had missed the night before. He wanted to share something from the day before that he hadn't had a chance to share.

After doing this for some time, I'm convinced we were created with the need to share our days with a circle of family and friends. Such a simple thing to do, but I believe the long-term results lead to relational, physical, emotional, and spiritual health. For this experience to be successful, parents must not use this time to scold or correct a child at the table who is sharing his or her day. To do so will certainly stop the flow of information during future dinners. Adults must not do this to each other either.

One night a week we have a biblical or spiritual discussion. For these special evenings we usually invite a family from our neighborhood. In the past we have used Pantego Bible Church's simple study guide to stimulate discussion around the Scripture passage on which an upcoming Sunday's sermon is based.[12] Everyone's ideas are heard, and gentle disagreement is encouraged. As a matter of fact, sometimes we invite half of the table to argue against the other side. By means of these wonderful discussions, the members of our family learn to think critically about how their faith connects with everyday life. This may be the number one legacy I leave my family—the legacy I hope they'll pass on to their children.

The meal is not over until the table is cleared and the kitchen cleaned. This ritual of cleaning does not fall to one person but to everyone who has partaken of the meal. It is a privilege and an extension of the festival. When this is completed, the mealtime is done for the day.

Under normal circumstances, it will take from 6:00 p.m. to 8:00 p.m. to have a meal (from the setting of the table to the end of the cleanup). We all await the dawning of a new day with the promise of its successes and challenges, all to be shared that evening at the convivium.

Open Time

Once the meal is completed, there are still two hours until bedtime (8:00 p.m. to 10:00 p.m.). Since work is not allowed, what is a person to do? Discovering what to do during this time frame each evening has been one of the most exciting changes in my life over the last five years. As a type A, hard-driving, boundaries-challenged person, I couldn't imagine not working on something. Here are the three rules to guide this final watch of the day:

- Do not do any work.
- Stay out of the car as much as possible.
- Keep the lights and noise low. God is getting you ready for a great night of sleep.

I have found the options endless:

- You can journal or have a devotional time alone.
- You can play a game as a family. We love playing a game on the floor while watching a sporting event on television.
- You can play a musical instrument. I love to go to my neighbor's house. He plays a folk guitar, and I'm a beginner banjo player. Sometimes others join us and sing along.
- You can listen to a CD on headphones.
- You can take a walk or pop in on a neighbor for a few minutes.
- You can sit out in the front yard if the weather permits and see who stops by.

- You can play a video game or watch a little television.
- You can read a novel or a good magazine.
- You can invest time in your hobby.
- You can dance with your spouse or child.

I don't know how you feel now that you've read this chapter. You may feel you have too many commitments to ever see this become a reality. Don't worry. In chapters 12 and 13 I'll make specific suggestions on how to begin making the transition. Right now all I want to know is if this is the kind of life and pace you long for? When I think of making room for life, this chapter describes what I wanted but found missing in my life. I hope it does for you as well. This is not a way of life for the wealthy. As a matter of fact, rich people seem to have the hardest time experiencing this kind of life because they have so many options to distract them. This is the simple way of life God intended for all of us. I invite you to come to the table and take in the wonderful convivium!

Before I began to add some reflections to each chapter of this book, I read the chapter and asked God to inspire me. Each chapter has been an adventure, and I have slowly pondered what he was trying to speak through me. This chapter was different. After reading it, I felt as though a holy fire was lit in me. I was so stirred I couldn't get to my computer fast enough. My sense of urgency stems from the experiences Randy and I have had since Making Room for Life *was published and we came across some new research confirming these experiences. As he mentioned, our family came to the convivium concept out of desperation. Yet, if we would have had any idea of the impact the family table can have, we would never have waited so long and perhaps would even have avoided our crisis point. My Italian heritage persuades me that, if I were sitting in a room with you explaining how important the convivium is, I would move close, gently take your cheeks in the palms of my hands, look into your eyes, and tell you there isn't one thing as parents you can do that will influence your children more than this. The very idea takes me back to my Italian roots, where life's pace is slower — people in small, pedestrian-scaled villages with cypress and olive trees, fresh pasta made daily, and families gathering every night for extended dinners together.*

If we can help you capture a vision for the influence the table can have on your life and that of your family, we believe it will radically change the way you do everything else. You will become so passionate about getting home for the evening meal that the Hebrew Day Planner will fall into place quite naturally. You won't even be tempted to go back to work after dinner.

The new information we've discovered about the ramifications of lifestyles starved of the table is chilling. The reintroduction of the daily table is revealing much more satisfying results than just filling our tummies and keeping us healthy physically. The far-reaching effects could change the course of our nation for the better — one family at a time.

The breakdown of the family has served to allow some ills of society to take hold like never before. Drug and alcohol abuse, violence among teens, teen suicides, and teenage pregnancies, not to mention ever-rising gang memberships, have brought heartache to many a parent.

Columbia University conducted a survey several years ago, and the findings may astound you as much as they did us. Researchers surveyed teens and parents trying to discover why some kids fall into drug and alcohol abuse, while others escape the danger. The revelation? The one big difference between the kids who do and those who don't is — are you ready? Having dinner at least five nights a week together as a family. Here is the information right off the pages of their most recent follow-up.

> *This year's study [September 2010] demonstrates that the magic that happens at family dinners isn't the food on the table, but the conversations around it. Three in four teens report that they talk to their parents about what's going on in their lives during dinner, and eight in 10 parents agree that by having family dinner they learn more about what's going on in their teens' lives. These conversations are key: Teens who say that they talk to their parents about what's*

going on in their lives over dinner are less likely to smoke, drink, and use marijuana than teens who don't have such talks with their parents.[13]

A leading factor in teens joining gangs is "a lack of friends or feelings of not belonging to a group or community."[14] They are searching to fill their God-designed connection requirement. Could it be that the disappearance of family dinners leaves our young people wondering where they belong? When our kids have a place at our table at home, the connection requirement is satisfied. What better parenting tool could we be searching for?

In a real sense, the table satisfies much more than our physical appetites. It gives a sense of well-being and security and satisfies our soul's requirement for connectedness. We don't believe it is "magical," as the Columbia University study suggests, but that it is mysteriously spiritual and goes back to our divine design.

Our desire as a family to return to the convivium was spurred on by desperation to overcome the frenzied rhythms of our life. It worked beautifully, but the research has shown us that the need and the impact go much deeper than we originally thought. If we start now as parents, we can see the next generation turn back to the convivium at large and have a great impact on not only our families but our nation as well. So, you see, it just may be that the hand that feeds the family rules the world!

Rozanne

As the Columbia University study suggests, it's not as important what is on your dinner plates as who is in the chairs. There are many convenient ways to cut time and still put good food on the table. If you must, grab a precooked chicken at the grocery store on the way home from work (it even comes warm), and open a can of green beans or make a salad. The most important thing is to sit down with your family and let them unpack their day for you, and you for them! For you empty nesters who question the importance of sitting down together to enjoy a meal, remember what Jacques Pépin declared: "Food, and the sharing of food, sustains human relationships more than anything else, including sex."[15] Turn the TV off and talk!

So as you get ready for dinner tonight, call your family around the table, perhaps invite a neighbor over, and meet around some Quick Chicken Soup for the Soul. Pop some Pillsbury Simply … Rustic French Bread (in the dairy case by the butter) in the oven to go along with it. It's the best and healthiest quick bread I know and has become a family favorite. Plan to linger around the table and share your days. After each person unpacks their day, have them rate their day on a scale of 1 to 10 (1 being the worst; 10 being the best). There is comfort in knowing that the people around the table love us so much that they'll be there for us not only on the good days but on the not-so-good as well.

Consider taking up this challenge: Simply choose one night of the week to share dinner around the table. The meal doesn't have to be fancy, but make sure everyone has cleared their schedule. It works best if it is the same night every week so that everyone counts on it. Try this for at least four weeks in a row. At the close of this exercise, I'm convinced you will look back and realize that the night you and your family looked forward to the most during those weeks was the evening given to the convivium — and I'm quite sure you won't want to stop. The future dividends may be the richest legacy you can leave for your family.

Quick Chicken Soup for the Soul

2 teaspoons of olive oil
1 cup of chopped onion
2 stalks of celery, sliced or 1½ cups pre-sliced celery
2 teaspoons garlic
7 cups of chicken broth
1 teaspoon ground black pepper
1 teaspoon poultry seasoning
2 cups matchstick carrots
1 (16 ounces) can diced tomatoes
1½ cups uncooked extra-wide egg noodles
2 cups shredded cooked chicken (can use 2 cans of precooked chicken)

Heat oil in large pan. Add onions, celery, and garlic. Cook two minutes at medium heat. Add broth, pepper, poultry seasoning, diced tomatoes, and carrots in Dutch oven (or large saucepan) over medium-high heat and bring to a boil. Stir in noodles and chicken. Reduce heat to medium. Cook for 10 minutes or until noodles are tender.

Yield: *8 servings*

Rozanne

|||||||||||||| DISCUSSION AND REFLECTION ||||||||||||||||

1. Think of one of your most meaningful dinners as a child or adult. Who was at the table? Was it a special occasion? What were you eating? Are there any common characteristics among your experiences of family dinners?

2. How many dinners do you share with family and friends in an average week? Are you satisfied with this number? What are the causes of your successes or struggles in this area?

3. The Hebrew Day Planner requires that everyone (adults and children) finish work by 6:00 p.m. Download the Real Simplicity App for your computer, phone, or iPad. Locate the Hebrew Day Planner calendar and plan your week on it. If you eliminated all office work, schoolwork, and housework, what are the top three things you envision doing with your free time after dinner?

4. Identify one personal action step you can take toward adopting a life of real simplicity.

The First Church
of the Neighborhood
Bringing Church Home

In 1990, I became the senior pastor of Pantego Bible Church in Fort Worth, Texas. My goal, with God's guidance and help, was to revitalize this struggling congregation. The counsel of experts and blue-chip practitioners at that time was to start as many programs as possible that would attract new people to the church. The logic was sound. Today's busy American shops for a church as a consumer, looking for the one offering the most options with the most excellence.

If you were to be a "church on the move," you certainly had to offer small groups, along with a myriad of other quality programs. So small groups it was. I operate on the principle of "speed of the leader, speed of the team." If we were to install this mammoth, leadership-intensive ministry, every staff member needed to get in a small group in order to model correct behavior. Therefore, it became a requirement for everyone on staff—including me—to be in a small group. Each year staff members would sign a covenant that included involvement in a church-sponsored small group.

So this meant I needed to join a small group. In the past I had participated in and led many small groups. But we were between groups, and this was a good opportunity to form a group that really ministered to Rozanne and me. I thought to myself, *I'm the senior pastor of the church. I bet I can recruit a stellar small group—the Mother of all Small Groups.*

The majority of American churches establish their connections in small groups based on a contractual theory. Simply put, it works something like a pickup baseball game. The two strongest kids are the captains. The rest of the children line up, and the selection process begins. How are members selected? From the strongest to the weakest. The same dynamic happens when forming small groups. We *contract* with others to be in our small group based on an upward association and invitation. In the end, these kinds of social contracts fail and lose their sizzle because they are contrived from the beginning.

Rozanne and I made a list of our dream team. These were some of the best individuals I'd ever met. To form them as a team—a small group—certainly meant we were the odds-on favorite to win the Little League World Series of Small Groups. Before we had our first group meeting, no one knew each other. We started meeting one evening every other week for about two and a half hours. I was fulfilling my covenant as a staff member of our church.

As this small group was forming, something else was taking place organically that I neither asked for, looked for, nor expected. At the time we lived on a street with about eighty houses on it. There were no cul-de-sacs, just a single street used by many to reach a main artery street. But the street had a certain charm. The neighborhood was developed in the early 1960s in what was once a thriving pecan orchard. We bought a small ranch house on the street. Not long after we moved in, a new neighbor moved in two doors down. I'll call them Kent and Susan. Kent and Susan had two children, were unpretentious, and didn't go to church. Kent was particularly gregarious. He would often meander over to the house in the evenings or on the weekends just to hang out for a few minutes or a few hours—I don't remember. I enjoyed his company.

On many Saturdays he took his newspaper and sat in our family room to read it. He helped himself to a cup of coffee or a cold drink from the refrigerator. Saturday morning was my lawn time. I put on some old clothes and leather gloves and got after it. The first time Kent appeared on a Saturday morning, I walked into the house for a drink of water and found him sitting on my sofa reading the paper. *Oh, no!* were the unspoken words in my head. *I have to host Kent instead of getting my work done.* I sat down and said, "So, Kent, hooowww's it going?" He peered over the newspaper and said, "I'm fine. Hey, isn't Saturday morning your lawn day?" "Why, yes," I responded. "I thought so," he said. "I do my lawn on Friday afternoon and like to relax and read the paper on Saturday morning. So if it's OK with you, why don't you get your work done and I'll read the paper, and then later we can catch up." It was music to my ears. I was out of there before he could get past one frame of a comic strip.

About a half hour later, I came back in the house. This time Rozanne was "hosting Kent." She had the same experience I did. As I went back outside, I thought, "How strange that he would come over to our house unannounced, help himself to whatever is in our refrigerator, and then not require us to host him!" It was strange, but I liked it—I liked it a lot. It was here that I learned my first principle of authentic community: *It breaks out when you can sit in a room together and enjoy each other's presence but not feel a need to always talk.*

One day, Kent came to my house to borrow a ladder. I was more than happy to oblige. A few days later, he brought the ladder back. About a week later, I was standing with Kent in his garage and noticed a ladder in the back corner. When I asked him why he had borrowed mine, he evaded the question. It was then that I learned my second principle of authentic community: *Drawing people into a circle of friendship involves not only helping out but also reaching out.* People want to know they are needed. Kent made me feel that I was being helpful to him and his family. I liked that feeling—and he knew it.

Kent and Susan introduced us to the neighbors across the street —a married couple with one child who was our daughter's age. They didn't go to church either. We began to hang out together, which was so easy, given that we were neighbors. Sometimes we would spend hours together. Many times our encounters only lasted for five or ten minutes as we left for work or took out the trash. Here I learned a third principle of authentic community: *It happens best when we spend frequent and spontaneous time together.*

Before I even knew how to define it or what to call it, these relationships expanded to others in our neighborhood and captured the hearts of our family. I distinctly remember the Friday evening when my wife and I drove down our street on our way to our church-sponsored small group hosted at a house twenty minutes away. We had hired a babysitter to be with our kids. We loved the people in our small group dearly, but with our busy lives we just couldn't get together outside of the every-other-week meeting. As a matter of fact, given the contractual theory of relationships, we still would have chosen them over our neighbors. But the proximity issue was starting to overcome us with wonder. As we drove down the street on a beautiful spring evening, the neighbors were out in their yards. We waved as we went by, wishing we could stay home with our children and neighbors. That's when the lightbulb in my head turned on. What if my neighborhood families could count as my small group? My heart leaped with excitement. I shared the idea with Rozanne. I could tell by the look on her face — before she ever said a word — that we were of one accord.

There was, however one problem: This would not qualify as a church-sponsored small group. "Wait a minute," I thought. "I'm the senior pastor. I can declare this to be a legitimate church-sponsored group!" And I did. Over the next couple of years, my team at church worked to understand the ideas behind this model. As we did, we gave ourselves more and more to the neighborhood. Here I learned a fourth principle of authentic community: *The contractual theory is not authentic, but the communitarian theory is.* This theory suggests that when we give ourselves to the people around us, even though there is diversity that we may not be attracted to, authentic community has a real opportunity to be experienced and found to be desirable.

Not long after the light came on in my head, Kent and Susan moved. We picked up the mantle and moved forward. As thirteen years on that street came to an end, our worlds had been seriously consolidated. While the neighborhood gatherings looked more like a scene out of *My Big Fat Greek Wedding* than traditional small group meetings, at the core there was a growing spiritual depth. A number of families and singles began to attend church with us on Sundays, but not all. Some went to other churches. Many came to put their faith in Jesus Christ; some did not. The experience was intensely intergenerational — from singles to married couples, from infants to senior citizens. For the first time in my life, my world of Christian fellowship merged with my world of relationships with irreligious people and seekers. It felt right — so right to the very core of my spiritual bones. (Reread chapter 4 if you don't fully understand what I'm talking about here.)

Twenty-some years later it's not only the core operating principle of my family's life — a circle of life — but it's the direction our entire church has taken. It took seven years for this to become a part of the DNA of our church. My commitment to this transition was so strong that I bet the farm on it. While we lost a few cows and chickens along the way, it was worth it. Today our church has place-based communities (neighborhood gatherings) all over our city.

Lyle Schaller, a wise sociologist and popular church consultant, said several years ago that "the biggest challenge for the church at the opening of the twenty-first century is to develop a solution to the discontinuity and fragmentation of the American lifestyle."[1] I strongly believe this simple strategy goes a long way toward solving this societal ailment.

Eight years later, my family moved about three miles down the road from our first wonderful neighborhood in Arlington, Texas, after much prayer in the bonds of a tight-knit community. The vision for this move was to take what we had learned and move into a new neighborhood to see if we could reproduce this simple idea. This time we wanted the community to have an intentionally spiritual foundation. So we decided to begin with this focus.

We moved into a neighborhood where several families from the church already lived. Our intent as we made this move was to stay home more and consolidate what it meant to be a follower of Jesus into this new circle of ninety houses. What Kent did in the last neighborhood was now my calling. We took walks, had neighbors over for dinner, and hung out in the front yard (weather permitting). We determined to stay with it and to consolidate as much of life as we could into this "circle."

Shortly after we moved in, we invited neighbors to a dessert get-together to explain our simple idea and ask them to consider partnering with us in this community life. We invited the families in the neighborhood that went to our church, families that attended other churches, and even a few families that didn't go to church at all. Would anybody show up? To our amazement, everyone we invited showed up! This was a good sign people wanted to know their neighbors.

At dessert time, we shared our vision for the circle of life. At the core we wanted to establish the presence of a Christian community in our neighborhood. While we would have a weekly gathering called "Home Group," we would all seek to do life together in as many ways as possible. We set out our covenant of purpose with an acronym that spelled S-E-R-V-I-C-E (the seven functions of biblical community):

SPIRITUAL FORMATION: We will help each other grow.
EVANGELISM: We desire for our neighbors to know Jesus Christ.
RECREATION: We will have fun together.
VOLUNTEERISM: We will volunteer to help our church.
INTERNATIONAL MISSIONS: We will help the church internationally.
CARE: We will care for each other.
EXTENDING COMPASSION: We will help the poor and needy in our community.[2]

We would not accomplish each of these purposes every week, but over the course of a year, we wanted to be able to point to tangible things we had done together to achieve our aim.

All the families that came to the dessert get-together were excited about the vision. All but one came on board. The family that didn't join us regularly attended Sunday evening worship at their church — and Sunday evening was the time we had decided we would gather as a group.

Over the years together, we've seen lives transformed. People have come to faith in Christ right in our neighborhood. We cared **(C)** for each other in many ways. We volunteered **(V)** for numerous community projects, extending compassion **(Ex)** as we shared the love of Jesus with those around us. We've ushered in the New Year together. We've taken at least a dozen vacations together. We've routinely had dinner together. We participated in international missions **(I)** by supporting a full-time pastor in India, as well as by raising money for Children's Bible Clubs for Indian children. Tuesday mornings the women in the neighborhood demonstrated a heart for evangelism **(Ev)** and caring **(C)** as they meet together to pray for the neighbors. Friday afternoons the men teed off at a local golf course, having fun **(R)** and getting to know the other men in the neighborhood **(Ev)**. The list of what we've done together seems endless. The powerful thing about this decentralized approach is that our church has given birth to more than a hundred groups all over the city doing the same things. This is truly the incarnational presence of Christ in a community.

How does a neighborhood gathering work? It's really quite simple. Luke describes it in the context of the early church:

> They devoted themselves to the apostles' teaching and to fellowship, to the breaking of bread and to prayer. Everyone was filled with awe at the many wonders and signs performed by the apostles. All the believers were together and had everything in common. They sold property and possessions to give to anyone who had need. Every day they continued to meet together in the temple

courts. They broke bread in their homes and ate together with glad and sincere hearts, praising God and enjoying the favor of all the people. And the Lord added to their number daily those who were being saved.

Acts 2:42–47

In the language of Acts 2, a neighborhood gathering involves breaking bread, enjoying fellowship, and praying together. Let me put it another way. Once a week someone makes a pot of soup, and anyone from the neighborhood, including children and senior citizens, comes and goes as they're able. During the course of your gathering, talk, pray, and plan together about what you could do to accomplish the seven functions of biblical community (see page 170). Because each neighborhood is comprised of a different collection of people, each group will choose different things to fit the makeup of the group.

If you want to start gathering with your neighbors, it might be fun to have a kick-off dessert and invite whomever is interested in joining you to read and discuss *Real Simplicity*. This will help people connect with the vision and decide if they want to become a part of what could become their "circle of life."

A few words of advice are warranted here. Don't push aggressively on these activities. Let the fellowship emerge naturally, and let each person give his or her input. Not everyone will participate in some of the things you choose to do. That's OK. Also, planning ahead is key. In my experience, a family typically doesn't take a vacation unless there's some advance planning. So it is with a neighborhood gathering. Finally, don't refrain from inviting unchurched people to your gatherings. Don't hold back from praying or from discussing your growing relationship with God. Just make sure that the people you invite understand that your gathering is faith based (note that it is faith based, not church based). Then if people from different churches or people who do not attend church come, there will be no surprises. I believe there is a longing inside everyone to connect with God and with a community. This may be exactly what they're looking for. In our Friday golf outings, one man brings a boom box and plays worship music, regardless of who is there. While it may be distracting for the golfer who requires complete silence, most people enjoy it. Lest you think that everything is a 24/7 religious church experience, it is just as common to get tickets to a concert and enjoy an evening of rock and roll!

As I write this chapter, four of the neighbors involved in our church and in our neighborhood gathering have gone on an adults-only vacation. Two of the families are empty nesters with grandchildren, and the other two families have kids still at home. We took care of their kids and dogs, watched their houses, got their mail, and did whatever else needed to be done. They do that for us when we are gone too. I'm sitting in my front yard writing this chapter. Any moment now, they'll be home. I can't wait to see them and catch up on the last six days. As I sit here, I've talked with ten other neighbors who have driven by or walked by. My children, who haven't been in any organized evening sports activities this spring, have been playing with the other neighborhood children for hours.

I have observed (from experience) that churches can complicate our already fragmented lifestyles. While spiritual nourishment and opportunity for ministry service are much more meaningful than most other things we occupy ourselves with, it seems there are better and simpler ways to go about it. For most people who live in the sprawl of suburbia, church is its own world—disconnected for the most part from our relationships at work, in our neighborhood, and with the schools of our children.

As I noted in chapter 1, church is not just one world but also several separate worlds. If you took the seven functions mentioned earlier (S-E-R-V-I-C-E) and created them into seven separate departments, you'd likely have a management mess on your hands. Typically, each area is managed by a different staff member or volunteer who doesn't necessarily coordinate with the others. Let's say you decide to be involved in three things because you really want to take your faith seriously. You sign up for a Bible study class that meets on Wednesday night; you sign up for the church softball league that plays on Saturday mornings; and you serve on the missions committee that meets once a month on Monday nights.

Let's say you are married and your husband joins a men's Bible study that meets on Thursday nights, and he volunteers at the church on Saturday on the landscape team. You have two children, one in elementary school and the other in high school. In addition to their Sunday activities, each one has a program on Wednesday night to attend. Without question, this is a lot of activity. To make matters worse, all of you are out of the house on different nights, and so you don't spend time together as a family. But another major problem exists: typically each of these worlds is disconnected from the other. Each time you meet you're dealing with a different set of relationships.

This is not bad in and of itself. The problem lies in the fact that this level of linear activity prevents you from having the time to invest in a circle of friends, which can help you meet the connection requirement. On top of that, these seven or eight linear church worlds are disconnected from the other worlds of everyday life that you manage! It is little wonder the average new Christian loses all contact with their non-Christian friends within two years of becoming a Christian and getting involved in a church.

There simply isn't enough time for everything and everyone. But what if we could naturally blend the world of church with everyday life? You and your family remain connected to your church, because it is important and meaningful to be involved in something bigger than one small group. Plus, the value that comes from corporate worship is irreplaceable.

This is the simple vision behind "The First Church of the Neighborhood." As you ponder and pray about the changes you may want to make, make sure you think carefully about this spiritual anchor of being in Christian community with others who live in close proximity to you. It's a crucial piece in the puzzle of real simplicity.

You may think you chose your house based on schools for your kids, the home's beautiful granite countertops, or its huge master suite, but we believe there is more going on than you know in the choosing of a home, especially in the lives of believers. In Acts 17:26, we learn that God chooses the exact places we live: "From one man he made all the nations, that they should inhabit the whole earth; and he marked out their appointed times in history and the boundaries of their lands."

Mmmm! Do you think he has a plan we may have been overlooking? He usually does. We need to discover what it is and then align our lives to his plan. The next verse tells why he determined where and when we should live: "God did this so that they would seek him and perhaps reach out for him and find him, though he is not far from any one of us."

God has placed us in strategic places so that people who live near us can find him through how we live our lives right in front of them. His greatest desire is to be near and have a relationship with each of us. God does not live in temples built by human hands (any more) but in each of us so we can extend his love to those around us. Is it any wonder God told us to love him with all our heart, mind, soul, and strength, and to love our neighbor as ourselves? His simple plan is to draw people to himself as we pay forward — right where we live — the love he has shown us. I don't know about you, but that gives me chills!

"Neighborhood life" happened to us and evolved into a way of rich community as refreshing as a cool glass of lemon water on a scorching Texas summer day. When we chose our house on Waggoner Drive in Arlington, Texas, we thought it was all about being closer to Randy's work. Yet there was much more about to unfold and impact us forever. At the time, we thought we were simply buying a house we liked. As a believer in Jesus Christ, I realize now there were many years when I did not even know, let alone hang out with, any people who were not believers and didn't attend my church. I just didn't have the opportunity — or so I thought. Perhaps you've had this same experience. Jesus told us to let our light shine before those around us so that they will see our

good deeds and glorify our heavenly Father (Matthew 5:16). It was years before we rediscovered that our light really does shine brighter in a dark world where Christ's presence is desperately needed, and much of the time we don't even have to speak a word. Our witness shines when we live in such a way that when others look at us, they see Jesus' love.

The church was never meant to be the proverbial "bushel" in the song "This Little Light of Mine." As you gather with others in your neighborhood who are Christ-followers, something unique happens. Christ's presence shows up, just as he promised in Matthew 18:20. When this happens in the neighborhood, it enables others around you to see and experience his presence in real and tangible ways. Unbelieving people see Christ's love when we love on each other and them. Our love for each other is often expressed behind the doors of the church building, where few non-Christians are present to experience this love and have Christ draw them to himself. Out where we live, we become the hands and feet of Jesus to each other and to the people in the houses in between. This is why, we believe, the first-century church enjoyed the favor of all the people (Acts 2:47).

We are now living in our fourth neighborhood since we began our quest for true biblical community and consolidating or simplifying our relational worlds. As we began our pursuit in each place, we learned much. The principles we began with have become honed. We have learned much from others who have come along and gone on this journey for themselves as well.

We have now simplified our strategy as a church. (Are you surprised?) Our Home Groups are now neighborhood gatherings, and they meet only once a month instead of every week. Yet, people are seeing each other many times in any given week. The foundational elements of these gatherings are now "Belong, Grow, Serve" instead of S-E-R-V-I-C-E (these seven elements are incorporated into the new categories, and we have a much simpler explanation of what people can expect). Neighborhood gatherings offer a place where we belong (more intimately than in the larger church setting), truly grow (because the relationships go much deeper in this "circle of life" than in the linear

worlds we drew in chapter 1), and serve together in the community
right where we live.

The gatherings are simple enough to include children of all ages. We
focus on the things the Acts 2 church experienced when they gathered.
We share a meal together, read a passage from the Bible, and have a
brief informal discussion (the kids play together, or they can join in
the discussion if they choose; the teens almost always join in). Then
we pray for each other and for the needs of our neighbors. We discuss
God's call to ministry in our neighborhood and beyond, and then we
pool our resources of time and cash to get the job done. This year our
group provided meals to those in our neighborhood who have been sick
or given birth and prayerfully supported group members as short-term
missionaries to Africa and China. A women's and men's Bible study
group emerged out of our neighborhood gathering. We went Christmas
caroling in our neighborhood to encourage some families that were
experiencing a tough holiday season. The possibilities for next year are
endless. Each neighborhood is as unique as the people who inhabit the
houses.

The coolest thing about each neighborhood is seeing a cross section
of spiritual gifts present in the believers God has assembled. We go
to our respective church buildings each Saturday or Sunday, but the
rest of the week we are the church. How fun to see each of these dear
friends share their giftedness with the group! Those who have a heart
for local compassion are coordinating our efforts as we reach out in our
neighborhood and beyond. We have an administrator who organizes
our monthly gatherings. Some of us host the gatherings (a potluck) in
our homes (the gift of hospitality). In the spring and summer, we gather
outside in someone's backyard or at our community pool. The reading
and discussion is led by different people who have a desire and a passion
for it (sometimes it is one of our teens). Teens and adults work together
to lead in a worship song as we open, and we take turns leading the
prayer time. How precious to think of our praises rising to God, and on
their way to his throne the sweet sound touches the ears of neighbors
nearby!

One key thing we have implemented is delegation. By not leading everything ourselves, it allows other people to take ownership and makes our work light. We know that if God removed Randy and me from our neighborhood tomorrow, the others would still gather and be the hands and feet of Jesus because they are accustomed to creating ideas for serving and having fun and are willing to step up to coordinate the group's efforts.

We typically kick off our neighborhood gatherings with a dessert social. We distribute fliers and see who shows up. We have grilled burgers and made pots of chili and boiled hot dogs. But no matter what we serve, when we've had our fill, we gather around and share the vision of the neighborhood gathering. From there it takes off. People in your neighborhood are craving connection and desiring a simpler way to do life, just as you are. They only need the spark to start the fire. When it catches on, step back and watch God work in and through your First Church in the Neighborhood!

Rozanne

If you are interested in the kind of community that will breathe new life into old wineskins, try this easy recipe for Chocolate Chip Pie. It is sure to please both kids and adults. Who doesn't love chocolate chip cookies? And this recipe is simpler and faster to make than chocolate chip cookies!

Chocolate Chip Pie

1 unbaked (9 inch) deep dish pie shell (4-cup volume)

2 large eggs

½ cup flour

½ cup sugar

½ cup packed brown sugar

1 teaspoon vanilla extract

¾ cup butter, softened

1 cup chocolate chips

1 cup chopped pecans or walnuts (optional)

Preheat oven to 325 degrees. Beat eggs in a large bowl until foamy. Beat in flour, sugar, and brown sugar. Beat in butter. Stir in chocolate chips and nuts (if desired). Pour into pie shell. Bake at 325 degrees for 55 to 60 minutes or until knife inserted halfway between outside edge and center comes out clean. Serve warm with vanilla ice cream or whipped cream.

Rozanne

############ DISCUSSION AND REFLECTION ############

1. Jesus wants us to experience rich connections with him and with each other. Why do you think that the church can often be more of an obstacle to community than a facilitator of community?

2. How many relationships do you have outside of your church weekend gathering? How many of these relationships are with people who are not Christ-followers?

3. Identify one personal action step you can take toward adopting a life of real simplicity.

Life Busters Part 1

Dealing with Sports and Homework

We have many opportunities and encounter many obstacles in our quest for real simplicity. I hope that by now you have a great attraction to the principles and stories presented. It probably makes your head hurt to think about all the changes you'd have to make to achieve your goal. No doubt there are some activities in your life that you know are enhancing disconnectivity, and yet you're not sure you want to give them up. That's OK. In this chapter and the next, we want to help you think through some of the most common barriers to implementing this dream. We'll call them "Life Busters." In this chapter we'll focus on children, and in the next we'll explore work issues.

When you're dealing with the need for change, you need to ask yourself *what level of change you are advocating*. There are three levels to consider:

Level 1: modest change—an improvement of the existing system

Level 2: substantial change—major change of existing system

Level 3: radical change—scrapping the old system for a new one

Not everything that needs to be changed requires a radical approach. Sometimes you just need a modest adjustment. If this is all that's required for effectiveness, then you should do it. Modest change is the easiest to implement and creates the least amount of conflict and discord. However, sometimes modest changes won't even make a dent in bringing relief to chaotic lifestyles. At times the situation requires a substantial or even radical solution. This usually takes significant courage and vision. Pioneers typically are not called pioneers because they approach life with a modest adjustment here and there. If you want to find a new way of life, it will likely require some substantial or radical action on your part.

As we look at the following common obstacles to achieving real simplicity, you'll have to decide the level of change to pursue. Place a check mark by the approach that makes the most sense to you.

Children's Sports

This area may equal or come in second to the automobile as the greatest obstacle to a balanced and simple life (see chapters 7 and 8). Children's sports programs are not bad in and of themselves. However, in the average suburb today, sports have taken over the evening and weekend hours and have kept the family in the car and away from dinner, conversation, and spontaneous play. Here are three options to consider:

1. ☐ **Modest Change:** *Sign up your children for sports with the children from other families in your neighborhood.* This plan gives you some options. When you are at a game, you can enjoy time with your circle of family and friends. You can even invite neighbors who are single or empty nesters to watch a game with you. For practices, parents can take turns carpooling and sitting at practices. Our family did this for years, and it helped. But for us as a family with four children, the plan didn't work over the long haul. The modest change didn't do enough to make it effective for our family.

2. ☐ **Substantial Change:** *Limit the number of sports and activities your children get involved in each year; select activities that can be done in the early afternoon, on Saturdays, or during the day in the summer.*

This proposal requires you to say no—and that is substantial. And this option limits not just the number of sports but the kind. Here the parent looks for sports programs and activities that are family and evening friendly when it comes to practices and games.

3. ☐ **Radical Change:** *Boycott organized sports until your children are in middle school.* For elementary-age children, opt for pickup games in the neighborhood or at a local park. By the time a child is in middle school, their coordination skills have developed well. Before that time it is debatable how much benefit in developing their skills children get from playing organized sports. Also, most schools own their own facilities, thus controlling the times of the practices or games. For the most part, coaches are teachers who like holding practices right after school instead of in the evening. This works well for families that value dinner together and settling down in the evening hours for conversation and rest. Of course, you'll need to encourage your children to discipline themselves to get their schoolwork done during the day at school or on Saturdays in order to stay in the sport. Otherwise they'll be doing homework well into the evening hours, and your family is back to square one.

This proposal suggests that physical activities and sports are appropriate for elementary-age children but that it doesn't need to be organized by a formal organization or league to be effective. When was the last time you watched four- to six-year-olds play basketball, baseball, or soccer? If you giggle as you remember this, you'll realize that it is a bit too much for them to handle developmentally. I'm also not quite sure if these young, highly competitive parents are ready for this high drama without embarrassing themselves on the sidelines. Type A parents should be required to take a class on sideline etiquette before their child is placed on a team.

I remember getting to the soccer fields early one day. I was glad to watch the game preceding my child's game without having to make an emotional investment. I watched one young dad walking up and down the sidelines and yelling at his kid. He wasn't the coach. I stood next to an older and more experienced dad by the bleachers. We gave each other that raised-eyebrow look, and he said, "This is his first kid in sports. He still thinks he's going to coach his son to be the next Pelé."

Here is an alternative: Gather a bunch of kids from the neighborhood (and maybe some of their classmates) for pickup games of flag football, basketball, baseball, kickball, volleyball, or whatever. These games are scheduled around the family's priorities and can prove to be as much fun as (maybe more than) organized programs. A hint: Let the teenagers help lead and coach younger kids. This is the option we've come to embrace.

We only wish we had had the wisdom and courage to do it ten years ago. (By the way, if your parents or in-laws have given this book to you — and you have children — this chapter may be the reason you received it.

Children's Homework

Homework is another opportunity and obstacle as we seek real simplicity. It is an opportunity because a good education is a worthy thing that will serve your children for the rest of their lives; it can be an obstacle when a child habitually has to do homework well into the evening hours. Remember that creating boundaries in your children's sports and extracurricular activities can help solve this issue.

This issue can be quite complicated because there are five major reasons homework can get out of hand: (1) The child has learning difficulties and struggles with schoolwork. (2) The child is involved in too many extracurricular activities. (3) The child is highly motivated to excel in academics and has "schoolaholic" tendencies. (4) The child is not using his or her time wisely at school. (5) The teacher is not effectively teaching the material.

Because of the variety of factors, these three solutions may not be adequate for you. Feel free to develop your own ideas and choose the ones that are right for you.

The Frazee kids were no exception to the general principle that kids hate to do homework. Here are some things we did to help make the chore a little less stressful for Mom and Dad as well as the kids, especially in light of the requirement that homework be completed before dinner at 6:00.

- Give up trying to make kids think homework is fun. Teach them that every job, no matter how much you love your chosen vocation, contains difficult tasks that, while not enjoyable, must be faced and brought to completion. The best approach is to dive in and get them done. Procrastination only drags tasks out and causes them to hang over you. Our goal as parents, in the end, is not to create excellent students but to help our kids become capable, well-rounded adults who can sustain themselves and give back to society.

- Collect cell phones before homework starts. Texts are a huge interruption for kids (and adults too!). After the first few difficult days of vocal opposition, you may find that they'll begin to see the benefit because they're getting their work done much more quickly. We don't recommend cell phones at the dinner table either (Mom's and Dad's included!), so why not keep them until after dinner? Oh, and whatever you do, remember that homework is not more important than dinner with the family.

- Find a clean, quiet place where your children have access to you should questions arise. Some parents like to have their kids do homework in their rooms, but we found this led to too much distraction for our kids. All four of our children did their homework at the kitchen table as I prepared dinner. I was busy enough to not be fully engaged, but if they had a question or needed to think through something, I was right there to help. We found that they were less likely to wander off task.

- Keep the perspective that no one excels in everything. If a child loves a certain subject, expect an "A" or "B," but if they hate a subject, be satisfied with a "B" or a "C." The only unacceptable thing is to not do your homework or not study for a test.

- *If a child has too much homework and is repeatedly hurrying through dinner to get back to work, it may be time to do some exploring. Sometimes a meeting with the teacher (along with your child) may be necessary to get his or her perspective. The teacher will be able to tell you and your child if any free time in class is being used appropriately. If the homework stills seems to be more than a child should have, and you've made sure your child is doing his or her part, you may want to express your concerns to the teacher (without your child being there), and then to the administration if you need more help. Be sure to approach teachers as though they have the solution to the problem, not as though they are the problem. The conversation will go much better!*

Rozanne

1. ☐ **Modest Change:** *Give your child an incentive to get his or her work done before 6:00 p.m. and to use Saturdays to get ahead.* Most schools give a child or teenager time to complete homework at school, but he or she often mismanages this opportunity. (This is totally human, since most adults do the same thing.) Reread chapter 9 on the ten principles of productivity and help your children apply these principles to their schoolwork. What a great mentoring opportunity for you! This, however, may not be enough. You may want to try a little incentive. Each night your child completes his or her homework before 6:00 p.m., he or she gets a treat or small allowance. Of course there are exceptions, such as studying for tests, working on long-term projects, and so on, and their grades must reflect that they didn't rush through their work just to get the treat. This practice is not uncommon in the business world. Many contracts are established with incentives to finish work early or on time.

Saturday is also an alternative to the evening hour. Remember, in the Hebrew Day Planner, Saturday is another possible workday—6:00 a.m. to 6:00 p.m. If you are Jewish or Seventh Day Adventist, you would use Sunday instead of Saturday as your workday.

2. ☐ **Substantial Change:** *Do the best you can to have your children do their homework before 6:00 p.m. and be open to B's and C's.* Children are wired differently. Some children receive A's while doing minimal work, while others work hard and long to receive B's or C's. Some kids just can't do as well in school as others. For some children, their learning styles may not match that of the typical school's teaching methods. Remember, success in one's vocational calling is not always determined by who gets the highest grades in school. As a matter of fact, sometimes the opposite is true. Success requires a balance in foundational liberal arts education; functional competencies in one's field of study; good people skills; a network; mentors; mental, spiritual, emotional, and physical health; motivation; and God's help.

If you feel you've taken a genuine crack at the modest level of change and didn't get the results you were looking for, you may want to move to the substantial change level. Several years ago, one of our sons was playing on an organized baseball team. One night we got home at 10:00 p.m., only to discover that he wasn't prepared for a major test the next day on Canadian history. (I realize it may be a surprise to some of you that Texans give any time to history lessons outside of Texas and the Alamo, but we do—albeit very little [just kidding].) My wife started drilling my son on endless facts and dates pertaining to Canada. By 11:30 p.m., productivity had reached an all-time low, and emotions an all-time high. Having quite a bit of experience with educational theories, I gave the two a much needed break and took a look at the material. This was education at its worst—an endless list of pieces of information without a good working knowledge of the big idea. Instead of having a wonderful understanding of the beauty, culture, and meaning of Canada's people and history, everything had been reduced to silly dates and unrelated, dangling facts. Instead of instilling a passion to visit Canada, I figured it would take several years of reeducation and therapy to get my son to want to vacation there of his own free will. At the end, my son had logged three hours of memorization, and I said, "Enough!" All this was going into his short-term memory bank for a test. In years to come, he wouldn't remember anything about Canada, let alone remember taking a class on it. We told our son to do his best, and we would all own and celebrate the results. What did he get on the test? A "C." That night at dinner my son shared these results, and we celebrated together. This was a major breakthrough for our family. A child should not be discouraged from getting A's, but under certain circumstances a lower grade may be the *smarter* option.

3. ☐ **Radical Change:** *Homeschool your children.* To some this will seem to be an extreme remedy. (That's why it's called radical.) Radical changes are a scrapping of the old or more common system for a new one. The key benefit of the homeschool option as it pertains to real simplicity is that it puts control back in the hands of the family. Many teachers today in public and private schools are faced with managing twenty to thirty children in a classroom, which converts much of the time that should be available for instruction to crowd management or "herding." This environment is simply inefficient.

As I researched the homeschool movement as a possible option for our children, I found three significant benefits:

1. Most children complete their work by noon or 1:00 p.m.

2. The movement has grown to include various approaches. There are programs that require the stay-at-home mom or dad to have a teaching certificate, but there are also programs that lay out all the lessons plans, use online distant learning technology, and even offer interaction with high-caliber certified teachers.

3. Homeschoolers can get a superior education. It doesn't take a rocket scientist to look at the academic results reported in reputable magazines to see that homeschoolers on the whole are outperforming those in institutional programs.

While there are many issues to consider before embarking on this journey, it is clearly an option if modest or substantial changes don't produce the desired results. The most important thing is that you are

Randy and I generally don't share our opinion on schools unless we are asked outright, and we never point to one option as the right choice for every family. But may I assume that if you picked up this book and are still reading, you want to know our personal thoughts? Each family, of course, must make the decision that is right for them. There really is no right or wrong answer, as long as you consider the needs of each child individually and keep in mind your ultimate goal of real simplicity.

Our family has taken advantage of all three schooling options. The majority of our kids' elementary school years were spent in private schools, which placed on us a financial burden, especially with college pressing in on us during the latter years. Rather than have Mom work outside the home or Dad take on a second job to pay the tuition, through many tears (mostly Mom's) we made the emotional decision to leave the only school we knew and opt for another alternative. Because I was afraid that my kids were not ready for public school, we chose to homeschool. When we moved to Chicago, we opted to send the kids to the public school in our neighborhood, which allowed them to attend school with students who lived around us and become connected more quickly with friends they would see often. Our kids did better than we could have dreamed. Our oldest son says that his one year in public school totally prepared him for college. Our second son enjoyed his new school even more than he did his private school. Let me quickly add that no matter which option you choose, you must be an involved parent.

We found several benefits in having our kids in public schools, among them being the fact that (1) our kids attended school with those who lived in their neighborhood and in nearby areas, which made it easier for afterschool play and cut way down on carpooling time; (2) we, along with everyone else, were paying school taxes — no matter whether our kids were homeschooled or attending private schools — and now we were reaping the benefits; and (3) the decreased financial burden simplified our lives so that we weren't constantly worrying about how to make tuition payments and pay all the other bills on top of it.

Rozanne

intentional and that you take action before your children are grown-up —and it becomes too late.

Without question, America has become a nation centered around child activity—carried out, generally speaking, for the welfare of the child. I'd like to suggest, however, that the overstuffed, overplanned, harried, commuter-driven lifestyles we are ingraining into our children are harmful. While our children should have lofty goals, dreams, and ambitions, they need a healthy lifestyle and healthy community in order to be able to achieve them. That's what this chapter seeks to encourage. Decide for yourself what action your family should take, and then do it.

|||||||||||||| DISCUSSION AND REFLECTION ||||||||||||||||

1. Look at the three recommended changes in the area of children's sports. What is your greatest fear if your family does not participate in organized sports?

2. As you think about schooling choices for your children, do you feel as though you need a change? Why or why not?

3. Do you sense that your children's homework is the right amount and in proper balance? What can you do to encourage homework to be done before dinner? Does the homework issue in your home involve a modest, substantial, or radical change?

4. Identify one personal action step you can take toward adopting a life of real simplicity.

Life Busters Part 2

Dealing with the Pressures of Work

We've stated it several times, but let's say it again: *Work is a good thing.* We have been created to be workers with a purpose. God works, and he has created us to do the same. The fruit of our labor is what God has designed to provide for our most basic human needs of food, clothing, and shelter. But the benefit of work goes even beyond this. There is a form of good stress, called *eustress*, that we all need for rich and fulfilling lives.[1] Work is one of the great outlets provided by God for this experience. However, we get ourselves into all kinds of trouble when we don't place boundaries on our work. Slouching over our desks, we find ourselves praying, *Dear Lord, help me to meet this self-imposed and totally unnecessary challenge.*

In this chapter I want to offer practical suggestions on how to keep work in balance with relationships and rest. There are five different workplace scenarios in which people often struggle to keep things in check: the two-income family, the single-parent family, entrepreneurs, shift workers, and business travelers.

The Two-Income Family

In my work as a pastor, I've found that ministry areas that excel are the ones that have full-time, motivated champions leading them. The same is true with managing a family and keeping everyone and everything in balance. If there's a full-time, motivated champion properly overseeing the homestead and family, there's a greater chance for success.

Raising a family takes time, skill, and intentional planning. Anyone who doubts this has never done it. In many two-parent families, both husband and wife work full-time jobs outside of the home, which pays the bills but also creates significant stress for the members of the family. If this is the situation in which you find yourself, consider the following suggestions:

1. ☐ **Modest Change:** *Be highly intentional and plan ahead.* If you sense there's no way to eliminate or reduce the second income at this time or you aren't willing to consider it, you must determine that your family is going to become highly organized and intentional. This involves, but is not limited to, having a strict schedule about who is going to be where at what time; what needs to be done at what time; when the family is going to have dinner; how the dinner is going to be prepared while everyone is at work; ways in which family members will equally share the responsibility. If both the husband and wife are going to work full-time outside of the home, then home management must be a fifty-fifty workload arrangement. Divvy up the responsibilities and hold each other accountable to get things done on time and within the boundaries so that you can have relational time with your family and friends.

2. ☐ **Substantial Change:** *Look for flexible work.* If you are convinced you must have the income of your spouse in order to meet the basic needs of your family but you desire to simplify your schedule and deepen your relationships, consider looking for a job that offers you greater flexibility. Look for a job that enables you to work at home or to adjust your hours (see my reflections on this idea in chapter 9).

3. ☐ **Radical Change:** *Downsize to fit one income.* As long as you're

not drowning in debt, it will probably take up to a year to implement this option for your family. If you've accumulated much debt over the years, it may take three to five years to achieve this goal. The main requirement here is to train yourself and your family to reduce consumption, to put a ceiling on your lifestyle, and to consider downsizing your residence and purchases. More and more people are making this move and finding great freedom in doing so as they discover that less can be more—less to pay for, less to maintain. They are also learning that less doesn't necessarily mean less quality, just less outlay of cash. If you purchase or rent a smaller place that has lower overhead in monthly payments (including property taxes and utilities), it doesn't take as much furniture and accessories to decorate it nicely. Our family has adopted the practice of "quality on a smaller scale." But there is much more to life than quality things; I've advocated in this book *accessorizing your life with quality relationships.* Here are a couple of questions to ponder: Do you want to work all day and into the evening hours to pay for a large home where you never spend any time? Or would you rather lighten your payments, and consequently your workload and stress, by renting or buying a smaller house where you can hang out with family and friends? After all, as we like to say around our house, "You can only be in one room at a time."

Many who read these words will feel as though substantial and radical changes are only for people with money. Nothing could be further from the truth. It is because of a lack of money that we need to look closely at these options and give up trying to keep up with the proverbial Joneses. We have certain expenses fixed in our heads as though they are necessities and rights rather than what they really are—optional amenities. This kind of thinking gets us into all kinds of trouble. Consider the surprising research reported by Cornell University professor Robert Frank:

> Whereas most families in the Gilded Age had to struggle to make sure their children were adequately clothed, nourished, and

sheltered, these needs are no longer at issue for all but a tiny fraction of today's families. The bottom 20 percent of earners now spend just 45 percent of their incomes on food, clothing, and shelter, down from 70 percent as recently as 1920. For most families, the current economic challenge is to acquire not the goods they need but the goods they want.[2]

The Single-Parent Family

As a pastor, I've never been more concerned for a specific group in my congregation than I am for the single parent. I've been married to Rozanne now for over twenty-nine years. We are on the same page in every area that matters. We are totally committed and full of energy, and yet it still takes everything in us to make life work. I can't imagine how single parents pull it off. The two responses I typically receive when I ask them how they manage are "by the grace of God," or "Pastor, we're not managing!" I've been inspired by a growing number of) single parents who have stepped up to the plate with a bat in their hands and are knocking it out of the park. What they've done is the only solution I have to offer. You can decide whether it is a modest, substantial, or radical change.

Get deeply connected to an intergenerational circle of Christian families that live in close proximity to you, preferably within walking distance. For many of us, extended family members don't live in the same town. If they do, hopefully you can rely on them to help out, but sometimes families aren't healthy enough to make helping you less stressful than doing it on your own. You must rely on Christian community for the kind of support you need, which is one of the reasons God has called us to community. Keep in mind, though, that this is not a one-sided proposal where the Christian community always gives and the single parent always takes. It is a mutual community where we help each other make up the difference when we come up short. It is the strong cord of three strands that Solomon said is not quickly broken (Ecclesiastes 4:12).

Entrepreneurs

The entrepreneur has the best of all worlds and the worst of all worlds. Entrepreneurs have it the easiest because they're in complete control of their schedule; at the same time, they have it the hardest because they're in complete control of their schedule. Because they are in control, they will have the greatest freedom to implement the principles of this book without delay or red-tape bureaucracy. However, most entrepreneurs love their work, and no one stands alongside telling them to stop. What's more, pure entrepreneurs don't know when they might get their next paycheck, so they never slow down. So, while most entrepreneurs have complete authority to gain real simplicity, most don't.

For the entrepreneur, I have two solutions to consider — one requiring a substantial change and the other a radical change. (I don't offer a modest suggestion because most of the entrepreneurs I know would never choose it, so why bother offering it?)

1. ☐ **Substantial Change:** *Adopt the "creation time management system."* God, the most successful entrepreneur ever, applied this system profitably. The principle is found in Genesis 1. Each day God focused on one thing, and once it was done he stopped for the day. On day four he said, "I'm going to create sun, moon, and stars today." On day five he said, "I'm going to create fish and birds today." On day six he said, "I'm going to create animals and humans." Similarly, it's a wise plan for the entrepreneur to identify a focus for each day of the week. For example, Monday could be "New Sales Leads Day." Have a 3 x 5 card ready with your top sales leads to contact. Get up in the morning and get after it: 1 – 2 – 3. When you're done with the calls, you're done for the day. Some days it may take two or four hours; other days it may take ten. Rarely, if ever, should you work past 6:00 p.m.

I have entrepreneurial characteristics, but I wouldn't consider myself an entrepreneur in the purest sense of the word. Yet, because I have flexibility in my job I've have found the creation time management system to work wonders. Here's my current workweek focus:

Monday: sermon day
Tuesday: development day
Wednesday: administration day
Thursday: staff day
Friday: day off (family budget time; recreation)
Saturday: optional day (home projects, occasional meeting, etc.)
Sunday: day off (except for preaching a couple of sermons)

Monday through Saturday I have twelve hours to complete the top priorities for that day's focus—things that only I can or should do. Once they're done, I'm done for the day. I usually check e-mails about three times a day (morning, lunch, and late afternoon). Some days I'm done in a few hours; many days I'm pressing hard to get everything done so I can be home by 6:00 p.m.

One thing that entrepreneurial coaches teach is that you need to have one day a week for administrative tasks. Entrepreneurs typically don't like administrative tasks, and so they tend to ignore these tasks, usually to their peril. OK, entrepreneurs, take out a piece of paper and play around with the creation time management system.

2. ☐ **Radical Change:** *Fire yourself (in other words, get a real job).* If you can't get your entrepreneuring in balance and you're stressed-out beyond typical entrepreneurial eustress, you may need to put your entrepreneurship on hold for a season. An *intrapreneur* is what I see myself as. I have entrepreneurial characteristics, but I work on a team and get a real paycheck every two weeks. There are two kinds of people for whom this may be wise advice: (1) true entrepreneurs who just can't get things going in this season of life or in the current economy—and they have a family and their life is completely out of balance, and (2) people who want to be entrepreneurs but who really aren't. Being an entrepreneur has been glorified over the last few decades, but it isn't that glorious unless you really are gifted at being one.

Shift Workers

If any shift workers are still reading this book, congratulations! The strict boundaries of the Hebrew Day Planner don't work well on second or third shift. However, if you have gotten to this point, I'm assuming it is because you believe in the concepts and principles but perhaps don't know how they can work for you. Let me offer two suggestions:

1. ☐ **Substantial Change:** *Do everything recommended in this book —but do it at a different time.* If you've read the previous pages, particularly chapter 5, you know that continuously working past 6:00 p.m. can create several long-term problems physically, emotionally, and relationally. As a matter of fact, new studies show that women who work the night shift have a 35 percent greater chance of developing certain kinds of cancers than those who work during the day.[3] However, if making a change is not an option, you should still seek to be intentional about relationships and rest. Take the three segments of a twenty-four-hour day (productivity, relationships, and sleep), and sit down with your family and friends and lay out a plan. When will you share a meal together? (Maybe it'll be breakfast instead of dinner.) When is the family's full day of rest if it is not Sunday? Which eight-hour block of time will be used for sleeping? While I'm not passionate about this option, I can say that working second and third shifts with intentionality and boundaries is far better than working these shifts without intentionality and boundaries.

2. ☐ **Radical Change:** *Make a move to first shift.* I hear you muttering under your breath, "Ah, the author has a great grasp of the obvious." Yes, it is obvious but hard to do. Some, not all, choose the second or third shift because it pays more money. I question if it is worth what you give up in exchange. I would rather have both spouses working than try to manage second or third shift with the rest of my life. The hard reality is that usually the family never completely adjusts to the shift worker's schedule.

If you embrace the principles of this book, you need to ask yourself these questions:

- What kind of changes do we have to make in our spending habits to pull this off?
- Where can we go to get out of this work cycle?
- What kind of schooling or training do I need in order to make a change to daytime labor and still earn enough money to provide adequately for my family?

Most careers—nursing, retail, and so forth—have daytime options that you might consider. For the last two years my daughter wanted to earn some money. She looked at working for a clothing store. We talked about it and mutually decided that she should target specialty clothing shops that close at 6:00 p.m. Monday through Saturday and are closed on Sundays. It has worked out beautifully. I don't think any store should be open past 6:00 p.m., and they should be closed at least one full day a week. (I'm guessing, though, that many people don't agree with me, since the "blue laws" regulating Sabbath behavior have been repealed in most areas of our country.)

My father-in-law was a successful independent grocer. He knew his customers and treated them with respect and helped them out when they were strapped financially. They in turn were loyal to him. The chain stores came rolling into town in the 1970s and stayed open seven days a week, twenty-four hours a day. They were obsessed with making money and didn't care about the web of relationships and community, even though their ads tried to suggest otherwise. I don't believe that people buy more just because stores are open around the clock. I just think we expand the options of when you can shop. For years I traveled through small towns where everything shut down at 5:00 p.m. In my ignorance I used to think, "What a podunk town! I could never live here." I was wrong. My father-in-law was wise enough to spot the trends, and he sold his store while it was still worth money. A few years after it was sold, it went out of business because it couldn't compete with the round-the-clock schedule of the chain stores.

I realize that there are some people who are genuinely called to vocations that require evening work hours. I met a lady who felt called to theater. I love theater and wish they only scheduled matinee performances, but if you feel that God is calling you to theater, you may not have another option. If God calls you to work a job, he will give you the strength to do it. However, you still need to be highly intentional about achieving balance between your work, relationships, and rest. Working evening hours may take its toll on your body over time, but if you believe this is what God wants you to do, then go for it.

I also want to be sensitive to the person who is stuck in a situation in which there are no apparent alternatives. These are not people who are making boat payments or wasting money on cartons of cigarettes. These are people who are ensnared in a vicious Catch–22 cycle. I'm thinking of the single parent who has a full-time job during the day and then waits tables at night to pay for medical bills and to put food on the table. She will not be able to get out of this downward spiral by herself. As I said before, this is a clarion call to action for the Christian church —a call to come alongside and connect and restore what "the locusts have eaten" (Joel 2:25). The church must connect this person to the kind of healthy Christian community that can help in a variety of ways —being with the children, making a home or apartment available at a reduced rent, providing financial support so she can go back to school and then get a job that pays a better wage.

Business Travelers

The final life buster to address is the issue of business travel. Many people in our congregation get on a plane on Monday morning and don't come home until Friday night—and they do it week in and week out! While this may work for a time for a young single person, over the long haul it eliminates all room for living. I'm not suggesting that business travel is completely out of the question, but it has gotten out of hand for many people today. Consider these options:

1. ☐ **Modest Change:** *Make trips as short as possible.* When I schedule a speaking trip (on the average about once a month), I look for two things: (1) Can I do it in one day, or no more than one night away from home, and (2) can I take my family along? I've found that if I articulate this goal up front, I can usually pull it off. However, when it's not a goal on the front end as the trip is being planned, I often find myself at the whim of others who don't necessarily take great care in navigating my personal life and health. Sometimes, when I simply must go, I sit down with the family ahead of time, and we make some intentional decisions to make up the time before I go on the trip. Sometimes I turn the trip down; I just say no.

2. ☐ **Substantial Change:** *Utilize technology to minimize travel.* With the rise of technology and gadgets, it often seems there is a better way to get things done than getting on an airplane and doing business in person. It's true that not all significant business relationships can be nurtured via e-mails and cell phones, but couldn't we at least cut the travel in half?

A few years ago, I participated in a satellite conference hosted by a popular writer and researcher. The broadcast had over ten thousand real-time viewers from all over North America. They could call or e-mail us, and we could interact with them. After the broadcast the host told me that he had talked with more people that single day than he would in smaller conferences in person over an eighteen-month period. With the rising cost of airline tickets, video conferencing is becoming an efficient and effective option for many businesses.

3. ☐ **Radical Change:** *Switch jobs.* Many people take jobs that require excessive travel because these jobs pay more money. But I think the cost is too high. Recently, I talked to a young married man with two small children who changed jobs to reduce travel, and he took a 40 percent cut in pay to do it. His comment on why he did it was insightful. He said, "My goal for taking the job [requiring travel] in the first place

was to earn more money and improve the quality of life for my family. This was an oxymoron. I was making more money and spending all of it, but it was drastically reducing the quality of my family time. I want to be around to see my family grow up, not just fund the family enterprise. I want to be in the pictures with my wife and kids—right in the middle. I want to be with my family and friends more, so I pulled the trigger and made the change—with no regrets!"

As the COO of our family, I have found time management principles to be invaluable as I execute my week. Most of the time, our jobs are ever before us. We don't leave our offices, and each day we see "another load of laundry" walking out of the house as those we love leave for school and work. It's almost easier for us to become imbalanced with work.

However, sometimes the biggest obstacle to adopting a lifestyle of real simplicity is—me. I am my own worst enemy. During certain seasons of my life, I have taken on part-time jobs with flexibility, as Randy recommends, and it has worked beautifully. However, when I wasn't working part-time, I found myself saying yes more often to ministry opportunities and Bible studies. I was busier than when I was working outside the home—but I wasn't getting a paycheck. I even felt pressure to take on more so I could "grow spiritually." I didn't want people to think I was lazy (pressure felt not only by pastors' wives but also by many stay-at-home moms). What's more, our belief system tells us that heavy involvement in church activities is more spiritual. This can and has become a "life buster" for our family—because when Mom (the bearer of major responsibility for the family's organization and scheduling) is consumed by other things, everyone is stressed.

Here's where I went wrong: (1) I cared too much about what other people thought, and (2) I believed I needed to prove my level of spirituality through service outside my family. I remember the day our women's minister came to me—an inexperienced pastor's wife—after I had turned down her invitation to teach women college students, and she challenged me: "As the senior minister's wife, Rozanne, you need to be mentoring the younger women in the church through teaching." Had God actually told her that? Was this my only measure as a successful pastor's wife? Why hadn't God shared this insight with me instead of her? *I sulked home depressed, feeling like a total failure. My response was not her fault. I needed to know that what I was doing was exactly what God wanted from me at the time, and that it was valuable. And I needed permission to stay focused.*

Through time and maturity, I gained a better perspective. Randy gave me his blessing and affirmed that I did not need to accept every opportunity presented. My family needed me to have a vision of creating a place in which all of us could grow spiritually and find real simplicity in our home. While I didn't accept that offer to teach younger women, it did start in motion a few years of trying to prove, mostly to myself, that I was totally devoted to God by serving in local church ministries. My schedule became overwhelmed with tasks requiring my attention long after the dinner dishes had been put away — and my family suffered. And men — this holds true for you as well. It doesn't matter how honored you are to be asked to serve on the church board. Don't let it take valuable time away from your family. They need you to be the spiritual leader there first.

As believers, we have to trust that our worth, our salvation, our self-identity are not up for grabs. Insecurity runs rampant within our circles, especially for us women. We all know that what God thinks is truly more important than what people think; yet we don't always live like we grasp the concept.

I have adopted several responses I force myself to use when I'm approached by someone to do something new — no matter how exciting it may seem at the moment (even if it is just an invitation to go out for dinner). One is, "Let me talk to Randy, and I'll get back to you." Another is, "Let me pray about this opportunity you're offering to me." Randy uses, "I don't have my calendar with me [he left it home on purpose — please don't tell anyone!], so let me check, and I'll have my assistant get back with you." If I'm sure an opportunity is going to gain a negative response I simply say, "This sounds like a wonderful opportunity, but it isn't within my area of giftedness," or "I just don't think I [we] could fit that into my [our] schedule[s] right now."

Two simple ideas have helped me over the years. First, remember that time not spoken for usually gets filled. I have found it helpful to schedule my weekly routine chores such as laundry, menu planning, and the like; exercise time; dinner prep time; time with my husband, time for our children; and time for replenishing and put it on my calendar and treat it like an appointment. Keep in mind that there is no redeeming the time once it has passed.

Second, serving in only one ministry outside of family and neighborhood is more than enough. As you simplify your life and begin to do life and ministry with those who live around you, time spent inside the church building becomes less. Time for ministry increases because it becomes a reflection of your lifestyle rather than "something you do" at the building where the church gathers on the weekend. My ministry at our church building is interpreting for the deaf. I serve on Sunday and rarely at other functions. For the most part, the rest of my serving happens in my home and neighborhood. Please understand that we are not saying you shouldn't serve in your local church body. We want to avoid vocational suicide and angry phone calls and e-mails from pastors all over the country! However, make sure that serving in the church is within your area of giftedness and is limited to one ministry and/or Bible study (two at the most). We strongly recommend identifying one area of passion and giving yourself to that. Yes, I am a pastor's wife who is giving you permission to say no to the harried lifestyle that the church can create. Remember, we don't go to church; we are the church.

Rozanne

There's so much more that could be said about work. We offer these thoughts on what we think are the top five life busters in the workplace. If your greatest struggle wasn't addressed, grab some trusted, well-respected friends and brainstorm the modest, substantial, and radical options with regard to your particular struggle.

Let us encourage you (*encourage* means "to put courage into"). If your work is currently out of balance and squeezing simplicity out of your life, a way to make a change to enhance your experience is likely somewhere on the horizon. The apostle Paul advises his readers, "Were you a slave when you were called? Don't let it trouble you—although if you can gain your freedom, do so" (1 Corinthians 7:21). Throughout human history most people found their options to be few. The Bible encourages us to be content in all circumstances (Philippians 4:11–12; 1 Timothy 6:6; Hebrews 13:5). We live in a unique time in history where numerous options are possible. While many have used these options to create greater disorder and imbalance, you can take the options and use them to gain real simplicity and make room for life.

Before sharing my next recipe, may I remind us of the importance of planning meals? This has probably been the greatest stress reducer in my life during the times I worked, and even when I didn't. Scrambling at the end of the day to figure out what our family will eat is like creating something from nothing. Only God can do that, and I'm not him!

Although it took some time to learn how to use my Crock-Pot and the Time Bake feature on my oven, it has proven to be an invaluable investment. Wake up in the morning and put in all the ingredients. Set the timer and the temperature and go off to work while your dinner is being prepared. I love multitasking! When I arrive home, I simply prepare a salad or a vegetable dish. My family is deeply grateful for these two inventions. We no longer end up with peanut butter sandwiches or hot dogs on a routine basis.

With a little planning—living by the Hebrew Day Planner, inviting neighbors over to experience real simplicity together—the dinner table becomes the destination of the day. It is the highlight of our family's day. The surprise may be how quickly your kids and husband start asking you, "What are we having for dinner tonight?" and "Who is joining us?" They will be looking forward to it all day. I promise that this is one of the greatest gifts you can give your family — helping them to live simply and bringing a fabulous end to their workday.

Pulled Chicken Tacos is a Crock-Pot recipe adapted from one that a friend used at our neighborhood gathering. I also included a great salad dressing recipe to complete your meal. Buon Appetito!

Pulled Chicken Tacos

3 pounds boneless chicken thighs

1 can (28 ounces) of whole fire roasted tomatoes

1 can (14 ounces) of crushed fire roasted tomatoes

1 can of chipotle peppers in adobo sauce (in the Mexican products aisle) (use one of these peppers and freeze the rest for later)

1 onion minced

2 teaspoons salt

½ teaspoon pepper

1 teaspoon oregano

2 bay leaves

Put boneless chicken thighs into Crock-Pot. Pour in tomatoes. Mince one of the chipotle peppers and add to pot with one tablespoon of the adobo sauce. Then add salt, pepper, oregano, bay leaves, and minced onion. Cook in Crock-Pot on low for 5 hours or on high for 3 hours. Cool and pull apart. Serve on tortillas with sour cream, cilantro, cheese, and lime juice.

Add a salad with Mexican salad dressing and some guacamole and chips, and you are good to go!

Mexican Salad Dressing

1 medium onion, chopped

⅔ cup sugar

1 teaspoon salt

½ teaspoon pepper

1 teaspoon celery seed

3 teaspoons prepared mustard

⅓ cup vinegar

1 cup canola oil

Mix all ingredients well in blender until smooth. Pour as much as you need over the salad and store the rest in refrigerator for another time.

Rozanne

|||||||||||| DISCUSSION AND REFLECTION ||||||||||||

1. Come up with one idea that could make your work situation simpler. Would you need a modest change, a substantial change, or a radical change?

2. How many ministry and service opportunities have you taken on at your church? Could you move away from a few in order to give you more time at home? Are you in more than one Bible study a week? Could you replace them with a Bible study in your neighborhood?

3. Identify one personal action step you can take toward adopting a life of real simplicity.

You Can Do It!

Last night, we had our annual Christmas gathering of our neighborhood faith-based group. This group has been two and a half years in the making. We had some fifty-five people (men, women, and children) join for a simple dinner of lasagna soup, bread, and salad. Then we traveled around the streets connecting our houses and sang Christmas carols to neighbors who have been ill or lonely or just needed some encouragement. We showed up at their door, sang four quick carols, and let them know we love them. One of the children gave them a gift—a plate of cookies or a plant toted around for just that purpose. I wish you could have seen the precious faces light up as we sang. I promise you it wasn't because of our singing; it was because the light of Jesus' love showed up as every door opened. As we have already shared and stressed, we know of no better way to consolidate your relational worlds and simplify life than through your neighborhood. It can be the greatest catalyst for your family to belong, grow, serve, and have the greatest chance for impact as you partner with other Christians who live near you.

I love the way Eugene Peterson paraphrases John 1:14 in *The Message*: "The Word [Jesus] became flesh and blood, and moved into the neighborhood." Wow, what a powerful idea! Jesus came from his Father's kingdom and lives in our neighborhood. Well, sweet friend, I'm here to tell you, if you are a believer, Jesus is alive and well and living in you! He hasn't chosen to live in a tabernacle, as in Old Testament times, or in a synagogue, as in New Testament times. He has chosen to live within each one of us. When you move into a neighborhood, he moves in with you. I don't know about you, but that gives me goose bumps.

It also brings new meaning to the story in Mark 12:28–34, where Jesus is questioned about which of the commandments was the greatest. Jesus replies, "Love the Lord your God with all your heart and with all your soul and with all your mind and with all your strength." Then he quickly added, "The second is this: 'Love your neighbor as yourself.'" Now that's simplicity!

If you don't know your neighbors, I suggest you put on a pot of lasagna soup (the easiest soup recipe I know) and invite some of them over tonight (OK, tomorrow night; I realize some of us are planners). But don't wait too long before you ring the doorbell and discover the story behind that door. Just get to know them. Let them see that Jesus' presence is in your house. Don't be surprised if sometime soon they ask you about your faith.

Take that first step toward simplifying your relational worlds, and discover the most beautiful consequences imaginable. It is truly the simplest way to live, and over time, ministry is easier and more effective because relationships are more frequently experienced and go deeper. Park the car, stay home, have a simple dinner, play in the front yard, take walks, chat with neighbors you run into or who walk by. Before long, you will begin doing life with them — sharing hobbies and meals, or even taking vacations together.

To those of you who don't like your neighbors, Randy and I offer one simple solution: Move! We are kidding to some degree, but none of us are excused from sharing with our neighbors the love of Jesus Christ we so graciously experience. If God is not calling you to move, then go ring a bell, because even the crotchetiest of neighbors will be transformed by the love of Christ.

Yes, Jesus moved into your neighborhood when you did. Have you introduced him around yet?

Rozanne and Randy Frazee

Lasagna Soup

4 pounds of ground beef

1 cup chopped onion

3 cloves of minced garlic

8 cans (14.5 ounces each) beef broth

4 cans (14.5 ounces each) diced tomatoes
(with basil and garlic)

1 teaspoon dried Italian seasoning

5 cups uncooked mafalda or corkscrew pasta

1 cup grated Parmesan cheese

Cook beef, onion, and garlic in a large soup pot or Dutch oven until browned. Drain. Add the broth, tomatoes and Italian seasoning. Heat to a boil. Stir in the pasta right before you want to serve and cook for 10 minutes or until pasta is done. Stir in cheese. Serve with additional cheese if desired.

This recipe can be made a day ahead, but do not add the pasta or cheese until just before serving. If you make the soup ahead of time and freeze it, wait to add the pasta until you have thawed the soup and are ready to heat it.

Rozanne

The Hebrew Day Planner

The Hebrew Day Planner is an ancient approach to real simplicity and offers great help for the harried American.

As you look at this sample planner, notice the evening time comes first. This may mess with your head a bit; it did ours. But try it for a few days. We hope this exercise will help solidify the importance of the concept.

Start on Sunday night at 6:00 p.m. and finish on the next Sunday night at 6:00 p.m. Be intentional about planning your day to fit into this schedule. You will be planning the end of your day first, which is your dinner and relational time—the time God deems most important. After a week of trying this, evaluate and see how you did. Decide if you think designing your days this way has merit. If it does, give it a try for another week. We think you will find that whatever you plan for the 6:00 p.m. to 10:00 p.m. time will become your destination. It may just become a way a life for you—a way of finding real simplicity.

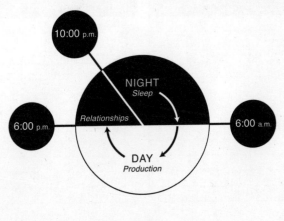

The Hebrew Day Planner

SUNDAY

Schedule for Sunday _____ _Date_

RELATIONSHIPS
- 6:00 p.m. *Saturday*
- 7:00 p.m. *Saturday*
- 8:00 p.m. *Saturday*
- 9:00 p.m. *Saturday*

SLEEP
- 10:00 p.m. *Saturday*

REST AND REPLENISH
- 6:00 a.m.
- 7:00 a.m.
- 8:00 a.m.
- 9:00 a.m.
- 10:00 a.m.
- 11:00 a.m.
- 12:00 p.m.
- 1:00 p.m.
- 2:00 p.m.
- 3:00 p.m.
- 4:00 p.m.
- 5:00 p.m.

MONDAY

Schedule for Monday _____ _Date_

RELATIONSHIPS
- 6:00 p.m. *Sunday*
- 7:00 p.m. *Sunday*
- 8:00 p.m. *Sunday*
- 9:00 p.m. *Sunday*

SLEEP
- 10:00 p.m. *Sunday*

PRODUCTION
- 6:00 a.m.
- 7:00 a.m.
- 8:00 a.m.
- 9:00 a.m.
- 10:00 a.m.
- 11:00 a.m.
- 12:00 p.m.
- 1:00 p.m.
- 2:00 p.m.
- 3:00 p.m.
- 4:00 p.m.
- 5:00 p.m.

TUESDAY

Schedule for Tuesday _____ _Date_

RELATIONSHIPS
- 6:00 p.m. *Monday*
- 7:00 p.m. *Monday*
- 8:00 p.m. *Monday*
- 9:00 p.m. *Monday*

SLEEP
- 10:00 p.m. *Monday*

PRODUCTION
- 6:00 a.m.
- 7:00 a.m.
- 8:00 a.m.
- 9:00 a.m.
- 10:00 a.m.
- 11:00 a.m.
- 12:00 p.m.
- 1:00 p.m.
- 2:00 p.m.
- 3:00 p.m.
- 4:00 p.m.
- 5:00 p.m.

WEDNESDAY

Schedule for Wednesday _____ _Date_

RELATIONSHIPS
- 6:00 p.m. *Tuesday*
- 7:00 p.m. *Tuesday*
- 8:00 p.m. *Tuesday*
- 9:00 p.m. *Tuesday*

SLEEP
- 10:00 p.m. *Tuesday*

PRODUCTION
- 6:00 a.m.
- 7:00 a.m.
- 8:00 a.m.
- 9:00 a.m.
- 10:00 a.m.
- 11:00 a.m.
- 12:00 p.m.
- 1:00 p.m.
- 2:00 p.m.
- 3:00 p.m.
- 4:00 p.m.
- 5:00 p.m.

The Hebrew Day Planner

Schedule for Thursday
Date

RELATIONSHIPS	6:00 p.m. *Wednesday*	
	7:00 p.m. *Wednesday*	
	8:00 p.m. *Wednesday*	
	9:00 p.m. *Wednesday*	
SLEEP	10:00 p.m. *Wednesday*	
PRODUCTION	6:00 a.m.	
	7:00 a.m.	
	8:00 a.m.	
	9:00 a.m.	
	10:00 a.m.	
	11:00 a.m.	
	12:00 p.m.	
	1:00 p.m.	
	2:00 p.m.	
	3:00 p.m.	
	4:00 p.m.	
	5:00 p.m.	

Schedule for Friday
Date

RELATIONSHIPS	6:00 p.m. *Thursday*	
	7:00 p.m. *Thursday*	
	8:00 p.m. *Thursday*	
	9:00 p.m. *Thursday*	
SLEEP	10:00 p.m. *Thursday*	
PRODUCTION	6:00 a.m.	
	7:00 a.m.	
	8:00 a.m.	
	9:00 a.m.	
	10:00 a.m.	
	11:00 a.m.	
	12:00 p.m.	
	1:00 p.m.	
	2:00 p.m.	
	3:00 p.m.	
	4:00 p.m.	
	5:00 p.m.	

Schedule for Saturday
Date

RELATIONSHIPS	6:00 p.m. *Friday*	
	7:00 p.m. *Friday*	
	8:00 p.m. *Friday*	
	9:00 p.m. *Friday*	
SLEEP	10:00 p.m. *Friday*	
PRODUCTION	6:00 a.m.	
	7:00 a.m.	
	8:00 a.m.	
	9:00 a.m.	
	10:00 a.m.	
	11:00 a.m.	
	12:00 p.m.	
	1:00 p.m.	
	2:00 p.m.	
	3:00 p.m.	
	4:00 p.m.	
	5:00 p.m.	

Acknowledgments

Some of life's greatest joys happen to us through no effort of our own, and before we know it they change our life so drastically, we almost can't remember how we lived before. This is how *Real Simplicity* came about for us almost twenty-seven years ago. So it has been our extreme honor and pleasure to be involved with this project. We can take no credit, but thank our God for bringing us to the realization that neighborhood is important and could simply bring us a more satisfying life than we ever dreamed possible.

We also thank God for the many people he has brought into our life to encourage us as we made the paradigm shift from chaotic to simple.

To our children—Jennifer, David, Stephen, and Austin—we are so fortunate to be your parents. Our passion to be with you never diminishes as we see God unfold a page of your story each evening at dinner! To Desmond and Gretchen, we thank God that he has brought you to our family and to our table. We look forward to hearing about your days as often as we can. You will forever have a seat at our table. To our granddaughter, Ava, you light up our lives with your vibrant personality and have added many giggles and memories around the table. Baba and Nona smile at the very thought of you.

To Al and Joan Bitonti, Rozanne's parents, for your love, patient mentoring, and example, we dedicate this book. To Randy's parents, Ruth Ann and Ralph Frazee, as well as our siblings and their families

—we are thankful for the memories and laughter and all the dinners we shared. We wish the miles that separated us now were less so we could spend more time with you!

To those who have dared to live with us in community, our neighbors—those on Waggoner Drive and Bay Club in Arlington, Texas; in the little village of Barrington, Illinois; and now in the Village Green neighborhood in San Antonio—we have been blessed by your involvement and love. Each of your names is forever engraved in gold on our hearts. It is through you and from you that most of the principles contained in this book have been learned, tried, and honed.

To Larry and Ann Ivey, who took an interest in this young pastor and pastor's wife—Larry, you were so much more than our dentist; you were our friend and mentor. We remember the day you were found standing by us when those around you weren't. Our hearts were deeply comforted and encouraged by you throughout our time at Pantego Bible Church! Ann, we are among many who miss you dearly since you went to be with our Savior forever. We are grateful that you took this young mother and pastor's wife under your wing. You saw so much more in her than she ever saw in herself. Your love, mentoring, and encouragement influenced our marriage, parenting, and ministry more than you ever knew. We look forward to the day we will see you again.

To two men who have consistently and lavishly counseled and supported Randy through ministry and life—Bob Buford and Mike Reilly. Thank you. Thank you.

To the people who have been there for us through thick and thin, supporting our family in many ways—the Reillys, the Guions, the Veigels, the Hilliards, the Ballows, the Tunes, and the Lawrences. We love you and thank you!

To our wonderful friends and partners, Max and Denalyn Lucado—we greatly appreciate your phone call to ask us to consider coming to Oak Hills Church. We have loved every minute of serving alongside you. To Steve and Cheryl Green—we value and appreciate your help and friendship in all our endeavors at Oak Hills and in publishing. To the great congregation at Oak Hills—you are pioneers ready to go and have stepped out way ahead. We are learning much from you as together we become "the body of Christ, called to be Jesus in every neighborhood in San Antonio and beyond." What an incredible ride! To the elders at Oak Hills (all sixty-one of you!)—we are grateful that you unanimously invited us to serve with you and are proud of the way you are shepherding our neighborhood and area communities through your wisdom, love, and care. To our staff at Oak Hills, who work tirelessly to encourage and support our congregation in transitioning to a life of real simplicity—we appreciate every ounce of gusto you give to this vision.

To those at Zondervan who have once again believed in the Frazees and invited us to be a part of their great organization—Alicia Mey and Michelle Lenger, thank you for imagining and proposing *Real Simplicity*. We are grateful to Carolyn McCready and Dirk Buursma, our editors on this project. You have been the best to work with. To Moe Girkins, John Raymond, Stan Gundry, Cindy Lambert, Joyce Ondersma, and Jackie Aldridge—once again we have been blessed to be invited to the table to serve with you. Thank you for the opportunity to encourage people to live life to the fullest, but to do it simply.

Notes

CHAPTER 1: Crowded Loneliness

1. Sally Weale, "Do you often feel ill on holiday … but never when you're at work? If so, you could be a victim of 'leisure sickness,'" *The Guardian* (November 26, 2002).
2. Robert Putnam, *Bowling Alone* (New York: Simon & Schuster, 2000).
3. Heard on KRLD News Radio (AM 1080) in Dallas/Fort Worth, Texas, 2002.
4. Robert Putnam, "Surprising Facts" (see www.bowlingalone.com).
5. George Gallup Jr., cited in Randy Frazee, *The Connecting Church* (Grand Rapids: Zondervan, 2001), 15.
6. See John L. Locke, *The De-Voicing of Society: Why We Don't Talk to Each Other Anymore* (New York: Simon & Schuster, 1998), 202–3.

CHAPTER 2: The Connection Requirement

1. Elizabeth Warren and Amelia Warren Tyagi, *The Two-Income Trap* (New York: Basic Books, 2003), 10.
2. Ibid., 6.
3. Rich Sones, Ph.D., and Bill Sones, "Strange but True: Selling the 'me' versus 'we,'" in "Star Time" insert, *Fort Worth Star Telegram* (May 9, 2003), 69.
4. See John Allen, "Ubuntu: An African Challenge to Individuality and Consumerism," *Trinity News* (posted April 24, 2002).
5. Cited in J. Y. Mokgoro, "Ubuntu and the Law in South Africa," paper delivered at the first Colloquium *Constitution and Law* held at Potchefstroom (October 31, 1997).
6. Sarah E.F. Milov, "Sociology of thefacebook.com," *The Harvard Crimson*: www.thecrimson.com/article/2004/3/18/sociology-of-thefacebookcom-at-harvard-fun/ (November 8, 2010).
7. Paul J. Rosch, MD, "Social Support: The Supreme Stress Stopper," *Health and Stress: The Newsletter of the American Institute of Stress* 10 (1997): 1.
8. Ibid., 2.
9. Ibid.
10. Ibid., 4.
11. Ibid.

12. Ibid.
13. Ibid., 5.
14. Ibid.

CHAPTER 3: The Secret of the Bedouin Shepherd

1. Cited in Anthony Ham and Paul Greenway, *Jordan* (Oakland, Calif.: Lonely Planet, 2003), 214.
2. See K. Abu-Saad et al., "Rapid Lifestyle, Diet and Health Changes among Urban Bedouin Arabs of Southern Israel," *Food and Agricultural Organization of the United Nations*: www.fao.org/DOCREP/003/y0600m/Y0600M06.htm (January 21, 2011).
3. Ibid.

CHAPTER 4: The Circle of Life

1. Paul J. Rosch, MD, "Social Support: The Supreme Stress Stopper," *Health and Stress: The Newsletter of the American Institute of Stress* 10 (1997): 1.
2. Cited in Paul J. Rosch, M.D., "The Health Benefits of Friendship," found in "Stress Reduction Effects of Social Support" informational packet (American Institute of Stress), 11.
3. Randy Frazee, *The Connecting Church* (Grand Rapids: Zondervan, 2001).
4. Rosch, "The Health Benefits of Friendship," 10.
5. Quoted in John Shaughnessy, "Lack Close Friends? Refrigerator Is Clue," *Louisville Courier-Journal* (December 2, 2002).
6. See Will Miller with Glenn Sparks, *Refrigerator Rights* (New York: Penguin, 2002).
7. See Shaughnessy, "Lack Close Friends? Refrigerator Is Clue."
8. *The Andy Griffith Show* (1960 – 1968) featured widower Andy Taylor, who divided his time between raising his young son, Opie, and his job as sheriff (and Justice of the Peace) of the sleepy North Carolina town, Mayberry.
9. Jacqueline Olds, MD, "The Healing Power of Friendship," *Bottom Line/Health* vol.11, no. 8 (August 1997), found in "Stress Reduction Effects of Social Support" informational packet (American Institute of Stress).
10. "The Proximity Effect," *The Vineyard Magazine* (September 2002), 14.
11. Ibid.

CHAPTER 5: The Hebrew Day Planner

1. Archibald D. Hart, *The Anxiety Cure* (Nashville: W Publishing, 1999), 100.
2. Peter Drucker, "The Next Society," *The Economist* (November 1, 2001), 4.
3. Ibid.
4. Cited in Judy Woodruff, "Millennials Study Captures Snapshot of Young America," *PBS NewsHour*, February 24, 2010.

CHAPTER 6: Getting Life Out of Balance

1. *The Legend of Bagger Vance*, written by Jeremy Leven (based on a novel by Steven Pressfield), directed by Robert Redford (DreamWorks, 2000).
2. Archibald D. Hart, *The Anxiety Cure* (Nashville: W Publishing, 1999), vi.
3. Paul J. Rosch, MD., "Social Support and Type A Behavior," in *Health and Stress: The Newsletter of the American Institute of Stress* 10 (1997): 6.
4. Hart, *Anxiety Cure*, 193.
5. Ibid., 197–99.
6. Ibid., vi.
7. Francis Bacon, "Of Innovations," in *The Essays* (New York: Viking, 1986), 132.

CHAPTER 7: Childhood: An Endangered Species

1. Rick Hampson, "Are they relaxed yet? Jersey town to find out tonight—Harried citizens take a night off," *USA Today* (March 26, 2002), 1A.
2. Cited in Rick Wolff, "Burnout Takes Out Many Young Athletes," *Sports Illustrated*, December 29, 2003.
3. See Sue Shellenbarger, "Kids Quit the Team for More Family Time," *Wall Street Journal*, July 21, 2010.

CHAPTER 8: The Lost Art of Play

1. Cited in Neal Kunde, "The Lost Art of Play," *GIGGLE Parents Guide* (2002).
2. Jane Morse, "Neighborhood Watch Programs Help Build Citizen-Police Trust," *America.gov*, www.america.gov/st/democracyhr-nglish/2009/March/2009031010 5536ajesrom0.331402.html (January 24, 2011).
3. Barbara Brotman, "Sit-Down Has People Talking in East Chicago," *Chicago Tribune*, August 9, 2010.
4. Paul J. Rosch, MD, "Stress and Children," *The Newsletter of the American Institute of Stress* 7 (1992): 2.
5. Valerie Latona, "Kids and Stress," *Healthy Kids* (February/March 1998), 22.
6. Cited in Ellen Parlapiano, "Simplifying Your Child's Life," *Healthy Kids* (February/March 1998), 24.
7. "Teaching Kids Table Manners," *Professor's House*, www.professorshouse.com/ Family/Children/Articles/Teaching-Kids-Table-Manners/.

CHAPTER 9: Ten Principles of Productivity

1. James Patterson, *Suzanne's Diary for Nicholas* (New York: Warner, 2001), 20.

CHAPTER 10: Discovering the Convivium

1. George Carlin, *Brain Droppings* (New York: Hyperion, 1997), 36.
2. Cited in Eric Schlosser, *Fast Food Nation* (New York: Perennial, 2002), 22.

3. Ibid., 3–4, 7–8.

4. Margaret Visser, *The Rituals of Dinner* (New York: Grove Weidenfeld, 1991), 266.

5. Deborah Taylor-Hough, *Frozen Assets* (Milwaukee, Wis.: Champion, 1998); Rick Rodgers, *The Slow Cooker Ready and Waiting Cookbook: 160 Sumptuous Meals That Cook Themselves* (New York: Morrow, 1998); Anne Chappell Cain, ed., *Cooking Light 5 Ingredient 15 Minute Cookbook* (Birmingham, Ala.: Oxmoor House, 1998).

6. William Shakespeare, *Henry VI,* part II, act I, scene 1.

7. Alda Ellis, *A Table of Grace* (Eugene, Ore.: Harvest House, 2001), 15.

8. Cited in Visser, *Rituals of Dinner,* 262.

9. Jacques Pépin, *Good Life Cooking: Light Classics from Today's Gourmet* (San Francisco: Bay Books, 1992), ix.

10. Visser, *Rituals of Dinner,* 263.

11. "Rules and Orders of the Coffee House," in *A Brief Description of the Excellent Vertues of that Sober and wholesome Drink, called Coffee, and Its Incomparable Effects in Preventing or Curing Most Diseases incident to Humane Bodies* (London: Greenwood, 1674).

12. For more information on this study tool called "The Scrolls," go to www.pantego .org.

13. The National Center on Addiction and Substance Abuse at Columbia University, *The Importance of Family Dinners VI* (September 2010), 5, www.casacolumbia.org/templates/NewsRoom.aspx?articleid=604&zoneid=51 (January 26, 2011).

14. Grace Chen, "How Is Your Child's School Confronting Gangs?" *Public School Review,* www.publicschoolreview.com/articles/112 (January 26, 2011).

15. Pépin, *Good Life Cooking,* ix.

CHAPTER 11: The First Church of the Neighborhood

1. In a speech at a Leadership Network Conference in Ontario, California, October 1998.

2. See Randy Frazee, *The Connecting Church* (Grand Rapids: Zondervan, 2001), 82–83.

CHAPTER 13: Life Busters Part 2

1. See Archibald D. Hart, *The Anxiety Cure* (Nashville: W Publishing, 1999), 21.

2. Robert H. Frank, *Luxury Fever: Why Money Fails to Satisfy In an Era of Excess* (New York: Free Press, 1999), 15.

3. Cited in Rita Rubin, "Night Shift Not Kind to Melatonin," *USA Today* (June 3, 2003).

Share Your Thoughts

With the Author: Your comments will be forwarded to the author when you send them to *zauthor@zondervan.com*.

With Zondervan: Submit your review of this book by writing to *zreview@zondervan.com*.

Free Online Resources at
www.zondervan.com

Zondervan AuthorTracker: Be notified whenever your favorite authors publish new books, go on tour, or post an update about what's happening in their lives at www.zondervan.com/authortracker.

Daily Bible Verses and Devotions: Enrich your life with daily Bible verses or devotions that help you start every morning focused on God. Visit www.zondervan.com/newsletters.

Free Email Publications: Sign up for newsletters on Christian living, academic resources, church ministry, fiction, children's resources, and more. Visit www.zondervan.com/newsletters.

Zondervan Bible Search: Find and compare Bible passages in a variety of translations at www.zondervanbiblesearch.com.

Other Benefits: Register yourself to receive online benefits like coupons and special offers, or to participate in research.

ZONDERVAN.com/
AUTHORTRACKER
follow your favorite authors